To Thank a River

to Lillian Dronen — 1996
Tori's wedding

Jean Clausen

Jean Clausen

Badger Books Inc.
P.O. Box 192
Oregon, WI 53575

Author: Peter Schilke's Grandmother

© Copyright 1996 by Jean Clausen
Illustrations by Katherine Coté
Editing/proofreading by J. Allen Kirsch
Published by Badger Books Inc.
Color separations by Port-to-Print of Madison, Wis.
Printed by BookCrafters of Chelsea, Mich.

ISBN 1-878569-37-6

Some material in this book is reprinted by permission of the Sauk Prairie Star and the Milwaukee Journal-Sentinel.

All rights reserved. No part of this book may be reproduced or transmitted in any form by any means, electronic or mechanical, including photocopying, recording or any other information storage and retrieval system without written permission from the publisher. For information, contact Badger Books Inc., P.O. Box 192, Oregon, WI 53575.

To my husband, Norm, without whom none of it would have been possible.

I would like to say thank you to my daughter, Juliana, for her assistance in the book's final stages; to the many ONNs (Other Nature Nuts), including my children as well as to the KPs (Knowledgeable Persons), some named and some unnamed, from whom I have learned so much; and especially to my teacher and friend, Sally Benforado. They have all helped to make my life on the riverbank rich and fulfulling.

Juliana, Pete Schilke's aunt.
Pete - Tori's husband

Contents

I. Work or play? 7

II. Summer business 14

III. Playing...22

IV. Beginnings 36

V. Sounds of spring... 41

VI. Birds of Summer 46

VII. More about birds 52

VIII. Winter birds 61

IX. Water birds 68

X. Flowers 76

XI. Trees 88

XII. The prairie 101

XIII. Animals 110

XIV. Sauntering 120

XV. Being 130

Epilogue..141

Bibliography 143

I.

Work or play?

At our home on the Wisconsin River bank, Norm and I never were sure whether what we were doing at any given moment was work or play. One sparkling cold January day, however, the lines were more clearly drawn. We were snowed in. Shoveling snow can certainly be called work.

There was no hurry for anyone to get in or out of our 500-foot-long driveway, now covered with about two feet of snow. LP gas had been delivered earlier in the week; no danger of running out of fuel. Wood enough for two or three days lay on the porch, and a big pile nearby only needed a little more sawing and splitting. The larder was comfortably stocked.

At our house, shoveling out the bird feeding area has priority after a snow storm. As he does every winter morning, Norm got up from the breakfast table and said, "I'd better feed the birds first." After shoveling his way from the door, he cleared the ground around the feeders, then filled them with sunflower seed. Last, he scattered a mix of small seeds for juncos, cardinals and trees sparrows, which prefer to feed on the ground. On a really snowy year, banks from three to five feet high build up all around the feeding areas, protecting the birds from frigid winds that blow up the river. A couple of abandoned Christmas trees stuck in snowbanks augment the shelter and add to the scenic effect.

The rest of the shoveling could be done piecemeal and spread out over a day or two if necessary, since Norm is retired. (When our grandson Aaron was two, his mother Karen heard him explaining to a friend, "My grandpa is an overtired doctor.") It didn't matter if the shoveling got finished today or tomorrow; we were not in a hurry to go anywhere. When I went out to help, Norm said, "Pace yourself, it's good exercise if you don't overdo."

I decided that baking a batch of bread would be my work. Baking is always a noble occupation for bad weather; the result is comforting to those who eat it, and the process makes the baker feel virtuous.

The high point came about half an hour after the golden loaves were out of the oven. The smell had been tantalizing us for an hour. At last Norm took the knife and very carefully cut a couple of thick slices to eat, still so warm the butter melted right in.

"My mother would never let me do this," I remarked as I took the first delicious bite.

"My mother used to say warm bread wasn't good for us," Norm replied, slathering his piece with peanut butter. Privately I felt he was desecrating my perfect product by adding anything more than butter.

We didn't have any human visitors while we were snowed in, but our bird friends were constantly with us. An eagle flew by several times, just to emphasize the fact that being snowed in is a problem that only human beings would allow to happen.

Norm may be the chief snow shoveler, but I am in charge of snow shoes. After the snow shoveling was under control, it was time to turn attention to the ski trail running around the perimeter of our twenty-five acres. We must have had two-and-a-half feet of snow on the level — more than we had ever seen out here — and quite a bit of it was light and fluffy. Skis would sink down in and get nowhere, so I tried snowshoes. They distribute the weight over a wider, shorter space. One does not glide on snowshoes, however; one plods or waddles.

As I worked my way around the trail three days in a row, I realized that grooming a ski trail was more of a job than I had anticipated. The first day I really sank into the snow and I felt as though I were lifting about ten pounds with each step. About every fifty feet I had to stop to catch my breath. I took forty-five minutes to go around half the trail. On skis the whole trail takes about twenty minutes.

The second day I didn't sink in quite so far, and only had to lift five pounds with each step. That was a windless, sunny day. Pauses to catch my breath, only every fifty yards this time, were a pleasure. I use ski poles for balance, even with snowshoes. During the pauses I leaned on the poles and admired the untouched whiteness all around me. Snow was still clinging to branches of a craggy river birch. Scrub oaks in the farther meadow were waist deep in snow.

Sun felt warm on my face, in spite of zero temperatures. Silence was broken only by the single call of a crow across the river, a dog barking somewhere, and soft twittering of juncos foraging for seed on weed tops poking out above the snow. The faint hum of traffic on distant roads emphasized my solitude.

Time for my ski trail grooming was almost cut in half the second day. On the third day I plodded around without the usual pauses. By contrast I thought I was going almost as fast as skiing. Finally all seemed to be in order.

I switched shoes, stepped into my skis and started out. The skis seemed awfully long, skinny and practically weightless. I'd forgotten how effortless it was. If I strayed from the packed-down track, though, my ski sank far down, so I knew that none of us would be skiing if I hadn't done the hard work of grooming.

❄❄❄

On a cold winter day, Norm likes nothing better than to get out with his chain saw and turn some of our dead trees into nice neat wood piles. We decided to call our wood stove Ernest. We chose the name because he's so much a part of the family and he seems to understand the importance of being Ernest.

Living with Ernest has its ups and downs. Or warms and hots, should we say? But not hots and colds; we're never cold with Ernest functioning. He is one of those super-efficient sheet steel numbers lined with fire brick that is supposed to hold a fire for hours.

We do have a furnace in the basement, but it seldom goes on because the thermostat is in the same room with Ernest. This is a combination living, dining and kitchen area. Ernest not only manages to keep this room toasty, but his heat goes around the corner into the bathroom and, to some extent, into the bedrooms. We like our bedrooms cool anyway. The man who delivers our propane gas has just about written us off.

We certainly save money by buying only enough propane to fuel our water heater. Whether the wood we burn is free is a matter of opinion. I think it is, because I see it growing and dying and being harvested regularly on our acreage.

Norm does not consider it free. There is the gasoline, oil and muscle power required to run the chain saw, not to mention the energy needed to cuss a little and get it started. Then there is the energy demanded to split, haul and pile the wood. And the energy required on a cold, windy day to venture onto the porch, bring in a few pieces and put them in the stove.

And of course, Ernest has to be treated right to remain warm and friendly. Forget to feed him or remain away from home for eight or ten hours, and he sulks. If he is neglected for twelve hours, we have to bribe him with kindling, paper and matches before he smiles again.

The time Ernest's personality really shined, though, was the cold winter day when the electric clocks stopped at 3:23 and didn't start again until the old clock that chimes the hours said 7:45. It was getting dark at the end of a short January day, and our cooking stove was electric.

I kept at my knitting until it was too dark to see and then lit the kerosene lamp and all the candles in the house. I was amazed to find that I could read by the light of our seven-branch candelabra. Of course, Ernest was pouring forth his usual warm sympathy, without any electric thermostat to tell him when to go off and on. That's another thing about Ernest — he's so constant.

There was hot water in the tea kettle, and I soon had potatoes boiling on the stove, along with a pan of our homegrown green beans from the freezer. I had planned to use my small electric oven to bake wieners stuffed with cheese, which of course was now impossible. But I improvised an oven by setting the wieners on a rack in a heavy cast-iron pan. Ernest came to the rescue.

The food took twice as long as usual to cook, while I was lost in reading by candlelight. When dinner was ready we opened the doors of the stove, put up the fire screen and dined by candlelight and firelight. That night Ernest really knew the importance of being Ernest.

❊❊❊

The annual Christmas bird count can be "work," depending on one's point of view. "Birders," as bird watchers prefer to be called, are an interesting lot. They come in all shapes, sizes and ages; they prefer old clothes and seldom leave home without a pair of binoculars in hand.

Every year at the end of December, about twenty-five of these birders gather in our living room to compile the annual Sauk City Christmas bird count. They are quite relaxed, some even drowsy, having been up since dawn to count birds all day.

Most have left winter boots and outer jackets near the front door. Heavy wool socks propped casually on some of the furniture don't necessarily match, and sometimes they have holes. Men's hair is tousled from being covered by a warm stocking cap all day, but the women have made an effort to fluff theirs up a little. Sweaters are gradually removed as the warmth of our wood stove begins to reach cold bones.

To Thank a River

How do we really know exactly how many birds live here? Well, the bird count has been taken for many years all over the country, and it's done about as scientifically as possible. A circle 15 miles in diameter surrounding the nearby villages of Prairie du Sac and Sauk City is divided into eleven segments. Each segment has one to three observers, plus two of us who watch our own feeders and acreage.

Some birds don't travel far, so those counts are probably fairly accurate. With eagles, gulls and ducks, it's an educated guess, always on the conservative side as engineered by Ken Lange, the naturalist who had charge of our count. "Where were you when you saw those six eagles? What time was it?" And he asks similar questions until his scientific mind is satisfied.

Eventually the count is tabulated. Eagles may be down, gulls a record high number. New species are sometimes added — one year a golden eagle and a glaucous gull. New birds must be documented by detailed descriptions or confirmed by another observer. Information is exchanged, and no doubt many of those present slip back later to the reported location to add a new bird or two to their life list.

Sometimes the weather is ideal — not cold, no precipitation, not even any snow to slosh through, with marshes frozen enough to walk on. However, the count goes on in all kinds of weather. Part of it is done by car, with the heater making one comfortable. But much is done on foot. There's no specific limit to the number of coffee breaks and lunch stops you can make on a bad day.

Norm and I have the easy part, counting the birds at our feeder from the comfort of a warm house. The others trickle in as it begins to get dark, thawing out over coffee, tea, cider and cookies. Some sit down quietly to figure up their totals, but as more and more people arrive, the house is buzzing with news of what's new and what's where this year.

Apparently that's what makes it all worthwhile. Many of the same people participate year after year. There are four counts in the Madison area, and Sam Robbins, a retired minister and full-time birder, has often gone on all four of them. That's dedication!

One year the count was held two days before Christmas. The day was very cold, but bright and sunny. As those who had been out listening and watching for birds all day began to come in at dusk, we expected them to be thoroughly chilled. Instead, they seemed comfortable, and their choices between hot coffee and cold cider were about equally divided. More than one birder was heard to remark, "It was just a beautiful winter day!"

Norm always enjoys a good story and, after all was tallied, he said, "I think we ought to have Sam tell about the Anna's hummingbird." Sam has been known to drive miles to observe a rare bird. So he, of course, was one of the first to arrive at the residence in Waukesha County where an odd hummingbird was still coming regularly to a feeder in late November.

The bird proved to be an Anna's hummingbird, seen only once before east of the Mississippi. Normally living in the Southwest, it couldn't possibly survive the winter here. After some negotiations, arrangements were made to capture the bird in a mist net. This was done just in time — at the beginning of a big December blizzard. The Anna's hummingbird is now comfortable in the Tropical Dome at Mitchell Park in Milwaukee. "He was a beautiful specimen, brilliantly colored," Sam told us.

After this story, no one seemed in a hurry, so we sat and visited a bit longer. I remarked to Becky Isenring, mother of two children and one of the last to leave, that I was surprised everyone didn't want to rush off and finish getting ready for Christmas. She replied, "Well, you know, people have their priorities. With some, it's birds."

❀❀❀

As members of the Ferry Bluff Eagle Council, our daughter Juliana, her partner Richard and I take our turns at the Lookout in Prairie du Sac so people can get a closer view of "our" eagles through a good telescope.

"Look at that! I didn't know they were so big." "Isn't that beautiful" or just plain "Wow!" are comments we often hear. The enthusiasm is contagious. One little boy shouted to his friend: "Oh, cool! Come and look through here." A 10-year-old turned around with a look of awe on his face: "I saw his beak and his eye!"

People come from all over the state and many from Illinois. One Saturday afternoon Richard talked to people from California, Pennsylvania and St. Louis. And there are always countless folks we don't have time to chat with. Juliana met a family from Sweden on one of her shifts. International visitors who are at the university are occasionally heard speaking in their native tongue as they wait for a turn at the scope. One woman was heard saying, "I came here thinking I'd be lucky to see one eagle. Three or four was marvelous!"

The eagles generally are cooperative. From two to four can often be seen perching, soaring or fishing within sight of the Lookout. Viewed from Water Street, the kiosk, with its big plywood eagles on top and dozens of people crowding the Lookout in their colorful parkas, makes a very festive picture. If it's sunny and mild, this is more pleasure than work. However, on a cloudy, windy day, standing out there for an assigned two-hour shift can become a chilling experience. Then it's work.

To Thank a River

Some years, getting the Christmas tree is more work than others. One year the grass was bare and brown, there was a fine mist falling and we wore rain coats. Daughters Kristin and Juliana, Norm and I wandered about among white pines planted about eight years earlier. Kristin said, "There's a perfect one — look how full it is. Let's take that one."

Norm replied, "But there's another over here I want you to see. It's even nicer." He led us all over about three acres of scrub oak and white pine, until we finally found one that all four of us could agree on.

The next year Norm scouted the same area. "There's not a single decent tree out there. They all have a gap of from one to three feet between the top whorl of branches and the next one down." All the heat and humidity of the previous summer must have caused that spurt of growth. Finally Norm hit upon the idea of cutting off the top whorl and wiring it further down, bringing the tree to our idea of what a Christmas tree should be like. Now he thought we could find one we could use.

On the day chosen for tree-cutting, the temperature was eight degrees below zero. Norm, Juliana, Richard and I put on down jackets, warm caps, scarves, mittens and skis. Armed with a small saw, we skied into the same scrub oak and pine. It looked like a fairyland.

Every tree was draped with white ermine. The brown grasses of fall were concealed beneath immaculate white. Pine branches buried their heads in snow in obeisance to the god of winter. Two adult bald eagles rose from trees near the river and soared off downstream.

A slight breeze off the river felt like needles against our skin. Somehow, we didn't take as long to find the perfect tree this time. The previous year's expedition was more comfortable, but somehow it was too easy. This was more like Christmas.

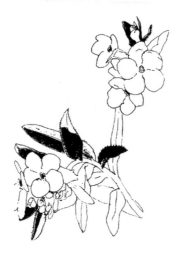

II.
Summer business

Come spring and summer, there's work involved with food. Let's start with our first crop.

It's a soft, early spring day, hazy sun, light breeze blowing from the south. The grass has been green for a while and it is time for my annual mess of dandelion greens. The leaves must be collected before the plants blossom or they will be tough and bitter. So I'll go to the north side of the house for my harvest.

It's a lot more work than getting a package of already cleaned spinach from the supermarket. And we haven't been starved for vitamins all winter like our pioneer ancestors. But the refreshing, slightly bitter taste of a mess of dandelion greens seems appropriate as a Rite of Spring anyway, to me at least. Norm won't touch them.

The dandelion's scientific name is *Taraxacum officinale,* meaning official remedy for disorders. Euell Gibbons, in *Stalking the Wild Asparagus,* says, "I don't think it is an exaggeration to say that this vitamin-filled wild plant has, over the centuries, saved a good many lives."

Maybe we don't need it, but I like to go out anyway on the right kind of day, and remove some of those "unsightly weeds" from the lawn. *Lawn* is a relative term. Norm doesn't fertilize or water — he merely keeps a small area around the house mowed, so we don't have to slosh through long grass in rainy weather. He also mows several paths, and a good-size area along the river at the foot of the steps —

for the same reason.

I don't dig deeply enough to get the whole dandelion root, but at least the plants I harvest won't blossom this year and spread their thousands of seeds about. They say the root makes a good vegetable in itself, peeled, cut crosswise thinly and boiled in two waters with a pinch of soda in the first. You can also roast the root in a slow oven for four hours, grind it and use it for coffee. I don't think I'll go that far.

After digging I carry the plants in the house, remove the roots and drop the leaves in cold water for their first rinsing. Until I learned that those are especially delicious, I also removed the tiny compact buds in the middle of the rosette of leaves. I rinse them in five waters (my mother used to say seven), picking out foreign matter each time. Even so, at the table later I still find a little stray grass. After washing the greens, I shake off as much water as possible and steam them in what moisture clings to the leaves for about five minutes. Once I tried seasoning them with butter and lemon juice as I do spinach, but there's plenty of natural tang to the dandelion greens. Lemon juice was too much. Now I use only a little salt and butter, or bacon fat if I have it.

Ancient herb doctors used the dandelion as an official remedy. As Gibbons puts it: "But how the mighty have fallen! The herbal hero, one of the most healthful and genuinely useful plants in the materia medica of the past, is now a despised lawn weed."

So I have my annual mess of dandelion greens. I wonder why they call it a mess? We don't refer to a mess of spinach.

❧❧❧

Another "free" crop comes a little later — asparagus. Our crop has dwindled over the years, but when we first moved here, an asparagus walk was my thrice-weekly ritual. It wasn't particularly productive; two small servings was the average take. But the taste of those lovely morsels, into the pan and onto the table within a half hour of picking, was worth it.

The asparagus walk included a glimpse of the delicate violet wood sorrel, just before the grass was tall enough to hide it. Or the flash of an oriole or a brown thrasher on the wing. Earlier in the season these birds came to me, near the feeder outside the living room windows; during the nesting season I must go find them.

One day as I started out on my asparagus walk the river stretched blue and calm on my left. I caught the flash of paddles in the sunlight, and the voices of laughing canoeists as they headed downstream.

I found two fat stalks under the big oak tree, my first stop. That's usually a good sign of more to come. Overhead a cardinal whistled loudly; he must be nesting nearby, perhaps in the prickly ash down on the bank close to the river. As I proceeded on the path along the river, I noted the tree swallow on his usual perch, a dead tree limb overhanging the water.

No asparagus on the next two stops; I guess the other plants have choked it out there. Spiderwort made the area on both sides of the driveway as blue as the sky. Next I heard the sweet, loud, long warbling bird song I had been hearing for several days — right overhead. Couldn't spot him for the heavy leaf cover. Could it be the warbling vireo? I know that species is practically anonymous, they're so hard to see. I stood a while craning my neck, to no avail.

Between stops number six and seven (five stalks between them) I spotted a vine with an unusual leaf. It was heart-shaped and had parallel veining. No flowers to help identify. Into the basket went a leaf for checking. Also a little yellow flower that looked almost like the violet wood sorrel, but with leaves more like blue-eyed grass. There were many, so I didn't mind taking a sample.

Back in the house, I checked flower guides and found that the tiny yellow flower is in the amaryllis family and is called star grass. The vine was wild yam. I wondered if it was edible, but since Gibbons doesn't mention it, I opted not to try it.

As I cleaned my asparagus, the kitchen window framed a view of my super-melodic bird in plain sight in the dead top of an oak tree, singing his heart out. Black head and back, white underparts and a large triangle of rose color on his throat — a rose-breasted grosbeak.

Not much asparagus, but what a productive walk!

❦❦❦

Zucchini is definitely work, both before and after harvesting.

One day I was complaining to a friend (or was I bragging?) about how much zucchini I had to use up or give away when we returned from a ten-day absence. She laughed, a bit smugly, and said, "Oh, the Z's have got you down!"

It turned out the Z's got to her, too, until they decided to put in only two plants, and that much they can handle nicely. You check the patch one day and find several pleasant-looking cucumber-sized vegetables hidden among the vines. The next day — especially if it has rained — they may have grown so large they scare you. Kristin, our botanist daughter, tells us their spectacular rate of growth is because of the high water content.

However, cooks have shown their usual versatility in coping with this productivity. One recipe that attracted our family is a zucchini patty with Parmesan cheese as a key ingredient. One afternoon I was frying several batches in my electric pan and conversing with the Drescher family, who were converging for an evening feast. Several recipes were discussed and exchanged, as well as other methods of disposing of zucchini.

"Most of the other people at the office don't have gardens," said Marcene, "so they're delighted to take as much as I'll bring."

I don't go to an office daily, so that wouldn't work for me. When friends take my offering, I'm never sure whether I'm doing them a favor, or they're doing me one.

On the day in question, Marcene, her daughter Becky and I shared recipes for cream of zucchini soup, zucchini bread, zucchini pickles, zucchini salad, zucchini casseroles (about six of these), stuffed zucchini and so on. Then Marcene's husband Bill arrived. He had come from their farm to meet the rest of the family here.

In a few minutes he turned to his wife and asked in a low voice, "Say, I've got the whole back seat full of zucchini. Do you suppose Jean would like some?"

❧❧❧

Then there is berry picking. You can pay to go and pick in someone else's patch or you can go find some wild ones and pick them free.

Strawberries come first, and those had better be cultivated ones. The wild ones are too small. At our place they are so small we can't see them. Every year we find large patches covered with white blossoms, but have yet to taste a berry. Oh, well, the birds probably need them more than we do.

It's good to hurry through breakfast on a warm June morning in order to arrive at the strawberry patch down the road early enough to get a good place to pick. Many other people are there already, with a mixed bag of containers, costumes and children. The old hands wear hats to keep off the sun, and long sleeves. The neophytes come in shorts and halter tops and go home with fresh sunburns. I wear my old painting jeans, so I can scoot along on my knees and avoid a backache.

The first picking often yields unbelievably large berries, "like the pictures in the nursery catalogues that you never quite believe," according to the lady in the next row. I usually bring home about six quarts for the family to savor.

Red raspberries also had better be from a farm or a truck garden. But black raspberries, locally known as black caps and, in August, blackberries, can be found in profusion in the wild if you know where to look.

Black caps were plentiful here one summer. Several bushes right at the top of the river bank, near the steps, were like another nursery catalogue picture. Some of the berries were green, some red and some purpling to their black sweet ripeness.

"Blackberries are red when they're green!" we used to chant as children. So are black raspberries — but their juice stains your hands red as you pick. Sugar them and serve them on ice cream and they leave blue juice in the bowl — and a wild sweet taste in the mouth.

Why is it so much more fun to pick wild berries than cultivated ones? The woods are quiet except for bursts of bird song now and then. Sun dapples through oak leaves overhead. The river moves inexorably and mysteriously on its endless journey to the sea. If you're hungry or thirsty, a handful of berries satisfies. You're feeding your family from nature's bounty — you didn't sow or hoe, you only have to pick.

But the best reason is that if you quit when you haven't really finished the whole patch, you don't need to feel guilty. You feel virtuous because you left some food for the birds.

❊❊❊

Work is also involved in keying out a flower. It's always a challenge, a bit like detective work.

One day when my ten-year-old grandson Peter was spending a vacation with us, he and I paddled across the river to a long sandy beach. At the upper end was a large patch of beautiful violet-colored flowers, on leafy stems two or three feet high. The blossoms were about the size of violets, which of course do not grow on sand beaches in August, especially on tall, leafy stems.

Since I didn't have a flower guide with me, and there were many of the delicate beauties, I picked one to bring home. If I find only one or two of a new flower, I always leave them in hopes that they will reproduce another year. Back at the house with the mystery flower, I began my search, like any good detective, looking for obvious clues.

One of my flower guides has charts to aid in finding out in which family your specimen belongs. If I remember to check the stem first, my search is easier; a square stem means the flower belongs to the mint family. This one had a square stem all right, but nothing I saw pictured on the mint pages resembled my blossom. Actually, it looked much like a snapdragon.

Back with the charts, I found that some snapdragons also have square stems. A monkey flower that looked similar had this notation: "July to September, six to forty inches; wet meadows, shores." That much was right. Next I checked my Peterson field guide for a few more details. I looked it up under the Latin name, since common names vary so much locally. It was *Mimulus ringens,* square-stemmed monkey flower in this book.

"Stem feels square-ridged," it said. The stem did feel square, but it was not a clean-cut square like the germander still blooming up on the prairie. The flowers were said to be borne on long stalks in the leaf axils; leaves opposite, sessile. (This time I didn't have to look up the word; I remember that sessile means without stalks.) Flower stalks, leaves, they all checked out.

Case solved; square-stemmed monkey flower. Like any good detective, I could relax now until the next case came up.

❊❊❊

It is possible to fake this flower identification business legitimately. Sometimes when I ask a knowledgeable person (KP) about a certain plant, he/she will reply, "Oh, that's one of the wild lettuces." This sounds so erudite that I don't ask more questions, although somehow it seems there ought to be a more specific answer.

Identifying plants is especially tricky in fall, when only remnants are left. One fall day when Juliana was living in Lafayette County, she came up with a puzzler for me. She brought me a fifteen-foot-tall plant with the remains of many small blossoms at the top. The leaves were thistle-like but not prickly. "I've asked several ONNs (other nature nuts) but no one has any idea. There were a lot of them this year, but none last year," Juliana told me.

Her specimen reminded me of a native plant called sow thistle which grows here — but is only about four feet tall. I looked that one up, but it had no really tall relatives. On the same page of my flower guide were a couple of those vague wild lettuces I'd heard about. They are listed under the daisy family, dandelion tribe. "Maybe that's it," Juliana said. "Earlier, it did have dandelion-like seeds."

In my Peterson field guide I found a long paragraph of explanation about the wild lettuces. One was called blue lettuce, scientific name Lactuca, with this note: "Much variation; critical identification highly technical." So I guess we can forgive KPs for not being more specific on wild lettuces.

Peterson lists three species, calling them all blue lettuce. The one designated Lactuca biennis grows fifteen feet tall, and is native to our area. Biennis must mean biennial and this did not appear last year. Another case solved. Now I could offhandedly say to any questioner, "Oh, that's one of the wild lettuces." Moreover, I can say which lettuce. I wonder if that makes me a KP?

Another fall activity that really is work: lots of oak leaves to rake.

Back in the city when the children were little, raking leaves was a pleasant chore. Each neighbor would be out raking on a gold-and-blue October afternoon. Dogs and children romped in big piles of leaves. The football game blared from a few radios, and loud cheers went up with each touchdown, blocked kick or other favorable play.

Then in the evening when the wind had died down I would hear, "Daddy, can we roast marshmallows?"

Norm and the children would go out to light the big pile. Marshmallow roasting was not very successful, but the delicious smell of fall would last into the light of the harvest moon.

Then along came ecology, air pollution, sensible fire regulations. No more burning leaves. "Wait for the city to pick them up." In the meantime, they blew back into the yard, or, if we were lucky, into someone else's yard. Some zealous people put them in plastic bags.

Where those leaves really belonged, this new thing called ecology taught you, was back in the earth to enrich the soil. But oak leaves were too acid and weren't good for the garden. So even on the river here, where we have a big garden, the oak leaves are still a problem.

One day I visited Sarah Longenecker at her summer home a couple of miles downstream. Her husband George had been a professor of horticulture at the university. As we enjoyed cookies and a cup of tea, I said, "Remember all those oak leaves we had to rake when you lived down the block from us in Madison? I thought that was a city chore — but we have just as many out here. What do you do with them? Oak leaves are supposed to be too acid for the garden."

"Oh," she replied. "George always saved his oak leaves. He added lime and fertilizer to the compost heap, and it made excellent soil for our sandy garden."

"Well, I'll try that," I said. "Everything must have been put here for a purpose, even oak leaves."

So on a bright crisp day I began raking in a protected area near the sheds where leaves collected ankle-deep. I soon learned to rake with, rather than against, the brisk northeast wind. Only three or four sweeps with the big rake, and my blanket was full. Gather up the four corners, carry the large feather-light load to the compost heap, and back again for more.

Such pleasant work, I thought, as I glanced out at the brilliant October blue river. The wind was hurrying the river downstream faster than it really wanted to go. In no time at all I had the area around the sheds all neatly taken care of.

But the compost heap was already more than half full of crisp, dry, very acid leaves. And there were about twenty times that many leaves, still waiting to be raked. I didn't look up in the trees, because I knew there were at least that many more that hadn't fallen yet.

Everything was put here for a purpose? Well, maybe some of everything.

III.
Playing

Our favorite form of winter play is cross-country skiing — but having enough snow is sometimes problematical. Twenty percent chance of snow predicted often turns into snow showers, leaving only a light dusting. After several such disappointments, on one lucky day, the snow showers kept on and on. Blackhawk Ridge and Ferry Bluff disappeared behind white curtains and soon fences and shed roofs were wearing fluffy white garments.

Late in the afternoon, the snow stopped. "Let's see if there's enough snow to ski," Norm suggested, pulling his blaze-orange winter jacket out of the closet.

I was ready in a trice. We stepped into our cross-country skis and set forth into several inches of powder snow, which is what skiers' dreams are made of. "We should have a base of heavier snow under the fluffy stuff," I said, but I wasn't really complaining.

There had been very little wind and small piles of snow lay in every conceivable corner and crevice. The bird feeder was wearing a white "curler bonnet." Tiny woolly teddy bears straddled fir branches.

Some dried goldenrod stalks were wearing Viking helmets, others wore Chinese coolie hats. The darker weeds had little white balls caught in their branches, looking like the cotton fields down South. Tiny seedheads of switchgrass, unable to hold any snow, were spun gold against the whiteness.

A faint rosy glow in the west told us the sun was setting behind that leaden sky. The river was wearing a gray satin dress and an ermine cape. As we turned toward home, a round golden moon moved in and out of clouds that were beginning to break up in the east.

When darkness finally fell, the sky was clear and the moon sent long shadows across the white earth. Every tree trunk and branch stood out against the background of sky or snow. The light of the moon made snowflakes sparkle at random over the meadow.

The whole thing looked fake, like a movie set. I wondered if it would be there in the morning.

❦❦❦

Indians had names for each full moon of the year: January was cold snow moon, February was hunger moon and March was awakening moon. We have an unobstructed view of them all from our home on the river bank.

One evening during the cold snow moon, thin clouds covered the stars and spread moonlight all over the sky. Norm and I put on our skis and headed along the upper river path. We needed no man-made light to follow yesterday's tracks. Wind blew sharp and cold from the north. Once down in the east meadow behind a hundred yards of river-bottom trees, we skied in comfort. Oak trees were bare, but globs of snow still hung on pine boughs.

"No problem seeing our way. Let's go on through the wildlife area," Norm suggested. Our skis sank through three or four inches of powder to glide on hard-packed snow. We heard only the swish of skis, the crunch of ski poles and occasionally the muffled sound of a car going by or the distant drone of a plane.

As we crossed the road into the denser darkness of a large grove of pines, I hesitated. "Won't it be too dark in the pines?"

"Come on!" Norm replied. The snow seemed to have its own light and we had no trouble seeing the path or each other. Patches of moonlight lay here and there on the snow. A little grove of aspens looked ghostly and unfamiliar as we came to the point where we turned back toward home.

Coming back across our east meadow by the middle path, we noticed dried stems of artemisia, graceful against the snow. The smell of wood smoke from our stove drifted out to us, at the same time as that knife-like wind off the river caught us again. Just then came the reassuring deep "Hoo, hoo, hoo-hoo-hoo" of a great horned owl across the river. Apparently he didn't mind the cold.

Over cocoa and cookies by the fire, Norm remarked, "Our friends who go South in the winter don't know what they're missing."

We knew what they were missing — the special magic of the

24   Clausen

cold snow moon or the hunger moon.

❧❧❧

Once we had a real old-fashioned winter. Even diehard skiers who usually hoard every inch of snow they can accumulate didn't object to the few inches that disappeared during January thaw. As for the rest of the populace, who could complain about three days of above-normal temperatures and sunny, calm days?

Oh, the thaw did louse up the skiing a little. Norm and I managed to ski almost every day, going early while it was still cool, or around sunset when the snow began to recrystallize. Sara and Jack Eberhardt came out with their skis late one afternoon. "Will the skiing be any good?" asked Sara.

"I'll go," I volunteered. "It'll be okay."

"I want to stay here and see how this football game comes out. It could go either way," Norm decided.

An apricot afterglow in the western sky encouraged the three of us as we started out. "We'll just take the short loop," I suggested. "Then it won't be too dark when we get back. The snow seems to have a light of its own as it gets dark anyway."

Ruts of previous tracks were deep, a bit icy and sometimes it was hard to stay in them. If a ski slipped out of the track, it went down six or eight inches because the deep snow was still soft. This had a tendency to throw the skier. I took a couple of spills and Sara followed my example once or twice, but Jack managed to stay upright.

In the pine woods where sun had not penetrated it wasn't too bad, but snowmobilers had been here and the tracks in the open were icy. I saw some inviting-looking ski tracks off to the left through deep snow that looked somehow more navigable. "I know where this comes out — on our regular figure-eight trail," I said confidently. "Let's try it."

So off we went, into scrub oak, across interesting terrain bordered by pines and crossed occasionally by animal tracks, very scenic in the deepening twilight. But these tracks kept going to the left, while the figure-eight trail was on our right. Once I thought I saw the trail about fifty feet away and tried making a new track in that direction. When we got there nothing looked familiar, so that project was abandoned. Getting back to our other trail was another matter. One of my skis came off and my leg sank in knee-deep. Eventually we managed to return to my "shortcut" and resume our wanderings. We could still see the trail ahead. Apparently the previous skier had not turned around, so he had to be going somewhere. But where?

"Here are some tracks going to the right," I finally announced, and we turned off. Soon we came to a wider trail with snowmobile tracks. "This is it!"

But I soon saw that this was not the figure-eight. Woods were thicker here and twilight continued to deepen. These ski tracks were more recently used, so I went on, pretending confidence that wasn't really there.

Eventually some pines loomed up that did look familiar. "This is the figure-eight trail," I said with relief. "But we are a lot farther back than I thought." At least we knew we wouldn't need to wander around in the Mazomanie Wildlife Area until dawn after all. Jupiter was bright in the western sky as we hit the main trail, but the fingernail new moon was not high enough to help light our way.

As we came out of the wildlife refuge we looked across the road to see that Norm had turned on all the outside lights. Only then did we realize that it was pitch dark. By feel and the luminescence of the snow we made our way to the door.

"No more shortcuts late in the day," I assured my guests. "Unless we can count on a full moon."

❦❦❦

A candlelight ski at Mirror Lake State Park! It sounded like the ultimate in cross-country skiing — out on those nicely groomed trails, led on by candles winding through snow-covered pines. Corine Hutter thought so, too, and invited a few Sauk Prairie friends (about thirty of us) to join her.

Fresh light snow came down most of the afternoon; three to five inches predicted. "Maybe the roads will be bad. Maybe we shouldn't go?" I questioned.

But Norm had no qualms. Our passengers, Marilyn VandeBerg and her sister, somehow arranged themselves among four sets of skis and poles in the back of our van. Snow slanting into our headlights brought back memories of driving to northern Wisconsin with children and weekend provisions in the station wagon, skis on top, and a feeling of excited anticipation inside the car.

Turning off the highway toward the park was like entering fairyland — pines embellished with white cushions of snow crowded in on both sides of the road. Then reality set in. "Look at that line of cars, just waiting to get into the park!" exclaimed Marilyn.

Finally arriving at the gate, we paid our day use fee and got some instructions and a yellow sheet of paper from a remarkably cheerful park ranger, considering that she was without a jacket in the frigid air. (Long underwear, no doubt.)

The first parking lot was full, and we probably got the last slot in the second one. Groping our way in the dark back to where we had seen a campfire and the beginning of a candlelit trail, we dodged other people and incoming cars. Near the campfire we wandered among shadowy figures, none familiar. "We'll just meet up there," Corine had confidently said.

Suddenly we heard "Sauk Prairie here!" and there they were. "Let's get going, we're getting cold."

We stepped into our skis and started along the trail at the end of the line. Parking lot cacophony disappeared. The trail wound gradually uphill through tranquil woods, pine and cedar boughs on both sides laden with snow. Our friends disappeared into semi-darkness. Little candles in plastic tumblers placed at intervals led us through a magic forest. Even out there, far beyond the candles' range, eerie natural light was reflected through snow falling from a cloudy sky.

I puffed a little, although Norm suggested I could be going a little faster. Great aerobic exercise, I reminded myself. My hands had been cold when I started out, but soon they too warmed up. No wind, ideal temperature — never have I been so comfortable outdoors on a January night.

Partway around the second trail we were no longer in nature's wonderful solitude. A single file of waiting skiers stretched as far ahead as we could see in the dim light. A traffic tie-up. Eventually it would be my turn to plunge into the darkness of the long downhill run, our reward for the earlier gradual uphill stretches.

Waiting didn't do much for my apprehension. What was out there in the dark? Would I be the only one to fall?

Apparently my skis found a good pair of tracks to follow, for I sailed smoothly down and back into solitude once more. We had a couple more traffic tie-ups before the parking lot could be heard and smelled. People preparing and eating winter picnics were busy at the campfire and at some charcoal grills. Our picnic was to be held at the Hutters', so we departed.

Arriving inside their Lake Wisconsin home, where we could see to read, we consulted the yellow sheets so thoughtfully provided by the park. "Always keep the candles to the right — this keeps everyone going in the right direction." "When night skiing, keep your knees slightly flexed. Stiff-legged skiers fall more." And so on.

Well, even without the directions, we managed to have a great time and not to fall. And down at the bottom our yellow sheet announced two more candlelight ski evenings. Now if we could just keep them a secret from the rest of the world.

❧❧❧

When we must abandon our skis, it is time to search for the first flower of spring. We had had our first rain and a couple of days of

To Thank a River

warm sunshine — winter was retreating! The East Meadow showed brown grass again; only snowbanks had failed to melt. Strong winds had dried up some of the mud. My friend Connie Peckham and her son Matt, who was then about two years old, were always up for an excursion. "Let's go look for spring," Connie proposed.

The earliest spring "flower" is skunk cabbage, which looks like a mottled, purple-to-green shell about four or five inches tall, with a pointed top. Peeking out of the opening is a ball-shaped spadix which contains the reproductive parts. Hence skunk cabbage is technically a flower although it doesn't look much like one.

"Where will we find this so-called harbinger of spring?" I asked Connie.

"It's always at Baxter's Hollow, as early as March," she said. Surely we would find it. We had seen other signs of spring: the first grackle poised self-importantly on the bird feeder; several wildly honking skeins of geese flying northward over the river; encouraging puddles standing in almost bare fields passed on our way to Baxter's Hollow.

As we turned off Kings' Corner Road and headed into the woods, however, we returned to winter. Bare spots were gone. Snow was more than ankle deep when we parked our car. Matt trudged along patiently in his blue snow suit and heavy boots. He had already learned that his mother's expeditions didn't always turn out as planned.

As we approached the bridge and turned in to walk along the stream, we plunged into snow over our boot-tops. The sun had disappeared in a bank of clouds. We had trouble finding a bare spot beside the stream to search for skunk cabbage.

"There's something red," said Matt. At the base of a tall oak he had spotted a lonely little partridge berry, bright red in its mat of round green leaves.

The stream, fast and full of the promise of spring, tinkled happily along. We found a dry log, then sat down to peel and eat juicy, sweet oranges, no doubt the high point of the day for Matt.

The woods were quiet except for the wintry call of a blue jay. Wandering back along the stream we admired the subtle greens of lichen-patterned rocks. Later we came across a little rivulet trickling over stones, bordered by emerald green moss. There was nary a skunk cabbage to be found in this last stronghold of winter.

Back home on the river we saw another skein of geese high in the sky honking its way north. "And there's the first canoe of the season coming downstream," Connie pointed out.

We were reassured. Spring was on its way, skunk cabbage or not.

❧❧❧

Some years it seems that spring will never come.

Imagine a gray day in early April, chilly wind from the east. Leafless trees, grass a halfhearted green, flower garden stalks brown and bent. "No signs of spring yet," said Norm as he settled down with the morning paper.

No signs? Take a solitary walk with me along the river bank. A cardinal is singing a commanding song from the top of an oak; that means he's preparing for the nesting season. From far across the meadow comes the soft song of a bluebird — one of the first spring birds to return here.

Juncos are still here, an indication it's still winter. But they are singing a contented little trilling song that we didn't hear much when it really was winter. They seem to be feeding constantly, probably preparing to leave soon.

A kingfisher scolds as he flies upstream, later returning to the area I was passing. Was he staking out territory that I encroached on? He may have been here somewhere all winter, but we hadn't seen him.

Near the river I find a tree with swelling buds. On closer examination they prove to be reddish, with a bit of green peeking out from their mysterious interior.

Graceful movement over the water catches my eye. Small birds with pointed wings fly in wide arcs over the river, turning occasionally so I can admire their snow-white breasts. If it were sunny I'm sure I'd be able to see how blue their backs are. Tree swallows — the first of the swallow family to return in spring.

Another harbinger of spring (that's a funny word — no one ever seems to mention a harbinger of fall) is the return of song sparrows. They are not singing today, but two of them have been feeding under our bird feeder quite regularly.

"Spring has begun!" I triumphantly reported as I returned to the house. "I saw a bright yellow patch of five prairie buttercups, just down that path. No one can argue with that."

❦❦❦

It is now a warmish May morning and I am sitting in my "warbler chair" under the oak trees. This is the only way I can enjoy spring warblers without getting a stiff neck. It's an ordinary lawn chair — the kind you can stretch out in — with the back lowered at just the right height to support my head and back while I'm looking into the tree tops.

Identifying warblers takes a bit of detective work. They move pretty fast and sometimes all you can see are the underparts, which are not usually pictured in bird books. Here comes one — yellow throat, yellow undertail coverts, faintly streaked pale breast, rusty cap, soft brown back. He wags his tail as he flits from branch to branch in the oak tree, foraging for insects with his thin, pointed beak.

While trying to follow him with binoculars, I also enjoy the soft yellow-green of tiny oak leaves and their matching lacy catkins against the blue, blue sky. We can admire the catkins now, but in a few more days they will be floating down to earth to clog our screens and require daily sweeping of porch and walks.

The tail-wagger I have just spotted is a palm warbler. We've also seen him foraging on the ground, although usually the best chance of seeing warblers is in tree tops. Here comes another species; he has a pale breast without any yellow showing, and he's not wagging his tail. I see a black eye line and a gray head, and no wing bars. These are important clues.

My field guide has two pages of warbler heads, one for those with wing bars and one for those without. This narrows down my search, and I conclude that he's a Tennessee warbler. I did notice, before he disappeared into the next tree, that he had a dark beak and legs. Some warblers have light-colored legs — another clue.

Next, another little bundle of energy catches my eye. He's shorter and rounder looking, and harder to keep track of as he hops from branch to branch. Warblers tend to work their way along one branch as they feed. This bird's behavior and shape tell me he belongs to a different family — kinglets. But there are two, ruby-crowned and golden-crowned kinglets. They are both dark gray with light gray underparts. I can see neither a yellow nor a red crown patch, although they are illustrated in the bird guide. Reading the fine print helps; it says the crown patches are seldom visible. What to look for is a white eye-ring, and it's easily seen on the ruby-crowned. A white and black eyeline would tell it was the golden-crowned. Both kinds pass through here, spring and fall.

More colorful warblers will be arriving in the next few weeks. The yellow warbler with his faint orange necklace breeds here. He's the only one that appears all yellow in the field. Another summer resident has a brilliant yellow throat and has a cheerful song that sounds like *witchety, witchety, witch*. Both can be heard singing here in the nesting season.

❧❧❧

The Wisconsin River is great for canoeing. One weekend in May, our old friends Oleta and Al Menzer arrived from Joliet, Illinois, to take a trip with us from Spring Green to Millville, the last canoe landing before the Mississippi. They brought Oleta's brother Bill and his wife Carrol.

Friday afternoon was pleasant under a warm hazy sun. Wild blue phlox and golden groundsel sprinkled riverbanks with color. A gentle breeze cooled us but didn't impede our three hours of paddling, although even with that short distance some muscles began to complain. Our campsite was on the right bank, not a sandbar. "But this breeze will keep the mosquitoes away," Al and Norm assured us.

When we began to put up the tents, I said, "Look at those tracks coming through the willows at the edge of the woods. Off-road vehicles use that path." The thought of moving on crossed my mind, but no one suggested it. We just didn't have enough energy to reload the canoes and start looking for another site.

The breeze died down, mosquitoes came and we all headed early into our tents. Al, Norm and I played cards, the others read and all of us went early to sleep. Before dark we heard the unmistakable *vroom-vroom* of an all-terrain vehicle. Eventually it burst out of the willows and zoomed around our sandy area quite harmlessly. It was a large four-wheel one with a canopy on top, holding a family out for an evening spin.

So far so good. But after we had fallen asleep came the midnight cowboys: three-wheelers complete with screaming girls reacting very satisfactorily as the drivers tried to see how close they could come to our tents. Fortunately after that it began to rain and we were able to sleep peacefully until morning.

The rain stopped in time to allow us to enjoy Al's pecan-and-banana pancakes and to pack up our mostly dry gear. A gentle rain began again, soon after we headed downstream. After donning our rain gear, we enjoyed watching raindrops dimple the smooth river as we moved past shadowy banks. Two sandhill cranes rose from one shore, alerting us with their curious croaking call.

We stopped at the park in Muscoda where the Mushroom Fair was in progress. I usually ignore garage sales, but Oleta and Carrol spotted one right away. "Look at these sweaters for a dollar," said Carrol.

"I found a pair of tennis shoes for fifty cents," Oleta said, displaying a pair that looked almost new.

Norm and I had grown careless about packing our gear carefully against rain and all that afternoon it rained harder. Everything was getting soaked and my raincoat began to leak. I was miserable and cold.

Eventually everyone was pretty wet, but we kept on paddling. "Might as well. It's better than putting up tents in the rain and then sitting around twiddling our thumbs," Norm said. Finally about five o'clock we found a suitable campsite, on an island where no three-wheelers could charge out of the wilderness. And... it was too cold for mosquitoes.

Mercifully the rain stopped as we were making camp, and everyone changed into dry clothes. But mine were all wet. I was most grateful for the warm sweater and dry shoes my companions had purchased at the Muscoda sale. Even our sleeping bags were wet, but again kind and better-prepared friends provided substitutes. Oleta lent me her own sleeping bag.

"I'm so warm-blooded I'd be uncomfortable sleeping in it on such a mild night," she said.

"Tomorrow's going to be hot and sunny," Carrol predicted. I didn't believe her completely, but it was. Not really hot, but the sun warmed us so we were eventually paddling in shirt sleeves. The beautiful part was a breeze from the northeast that often boosted our paddling efforts. Carrol and Bill put up a big umbrella and sailed a while.

The current was strong, too, and sped us on our way. We had traveled so far on Saturday that we were able to loaf along on Sunday to the Millville landing where we were to be picked up in late afternoon.

The bird symphony was out in full force after the soaking rain. Orioles, rose-breasted grosbeaks, song sparrows, phoebes, cardinals, yellow-throats — the chorus never stopped. Every shade of green graced the luxuriant river bluffs as we floated by. "The greens are more varied and prettier now than they will be in summer," Bill commented.

We had accepted Saturday's challenge; we were dried out, and Sunday was what all termed a perfect day on the river. It was almost worth it.

❄❄❄

Sometimes we prefer to be in the river instead of on it. My daily ritual is a refreshing swim — in season. The first year, we discovered that swimming in a river is quite different than swimming in a lake. The current is one factor, and the changing river bottom is another. We learned early never to fight the current; if in trouble, swim toward shore in a downstream direction.

I used to walk as far up as I could without getting into prickly ash on shore, then swim downstream for my daily exercise, clambering out on the neighbor's pier to walk back home.

As I came up from my swim one day, I interrupted Norm mowing the lawn. During his years of active practice, he emphasized preventive medicine, especially the importance of aerobic exercise.

"Take my pulse," I demanded. "Did I get my heart rate up

enough?"

"Ninety-six," he told me. "That's very good."

"I figured out that swimming across the current or against it is much better exercise and more invigorating than letting it carry me downstream while I'm just keeping myself afloat."

I chose what has remained a pretty good swimming hole over the years, about thirty yards upstream. It is deep close to shore and has a small sandy beach. Since I can't measure my laps by the number of yards I'm swimming, I count the strokes — back, side, crawl and breast strokes. I check my position with a fallen tree on shore, where I've hung my towel, and manage to come back in at the same sandy beach.

My daily swim refreshes my soul as well as my body, which seems to have a golden tan as I slide along under the brown river water. As I look upstream the water is a dusky, blue-green nearby; farther beyond it is almost bluebird-blue, crowned with golden sand where the river makes a bend. Above the sand I see the summer green of soft maples and oaks, and then the hazy blue of the Baraboo Bluffs. The hills are topped by a pale blue sky, which gradually deepens to the same blue it has bestowed on the river.

As I head for shore, I can see the house and flags flying from their pole on the bank. But they look unreal. For these brief moments I don't belong up there. I am a part of the earth, sky and water.

❦❦❦

When their daughters were about five and six years old, Jim and Kay Lindblade were visiting one weekend. We decided on an unusual way to beat the 97-degree heat — to go out in the full sun on inner tubes in the river. This may be hard to believe, but within an hour we were to find ourselves getting chilled.

"Be careful under the railroad bridge," Norm had warned us as he put us in near the Highway 12 bridge in Sauk City, about four miles above our place. Our conveyances were an air mattress and three inner tubes — one small, one medium-sized and one huge. We changed craft occasionally, but most of the time I had one of the inner tubes. Jim tied ropes from himself to both girls, their little blonde heads bobbing above the smaller inner tubes.

I concluded that an inner tube is a better vehicle than an air mattress (my previous favorite) because it is more responsive to the current. I enjoyed lying back to just see where I went. The others did some paddling with their hands to guide them where the going looked safest.

It was exciting passing under the railroad bridge. I let the current take me and for a while I seemed to be heading right into the left bank, rising several hundred feet above the bridge. Then I changed course and went faster and faster only about ten feet out from shore, apparently headed straight for an enormous cement bridge piling. When about five feet away, I was smoothly and safely ushered to the left.

My current took me around a sand and willow island, but the rest of the party were about to go down the other side. "Aren't you coming this way?" they called.

"See you on the other side," I replied. I couldn't have bucked that current if I'd tried. The railroad bridge has become more dangerous over the years and I wouldn't attempt it on an inner tube now.

Suddenly I was in a different world. Wild wooded shore to my left. On my right, broad sweep of wind-sculptured sand crowned by low willows and young aspen. No visible people. As a matter of fact, none of us saw any people for about two miles. The inner tube-raft entourage appeared at the end of the island and we proceeded with varying degrees of togetherness.

The wind was strong, coming upstream at us, and sometimes we had to paddle or walk to make progress. At other times we were in the main current, carried along effortlessly at a good clip. We could lean back and watch golden-tipped grasses dancing on the sandy shore or look up into a fathomless blue bowl of sky, sometimes decorated with white china figurines or wisps of cotton batten.

Occasionally half-hidden logs surprised us; we had to paddle furiously to get around them. We came very close to turtles sunning themselves on logs. For a brief stretch the wind was so strong it produced real waves a foot high and we were rocked as in a cradle. Eventually the wind blowing through our wet swimming suits made goose bumps form. "Let's land on that long sandbar and warm up," Jim suggested.

Finally the flags and the house appeared. The Drescher family had arrived and wasted no time in putting on swim suits, trying to cool off. They didn't believe our goose bumps.

❅❅❅

Sandhill cranes gather in large flocks just before flying south for the winter. One October day, Kristin and I decided to visit the staging area our friend Matt Millen had discovered on an island in the river near his farm.

Matt runs the family roofing business in Milwaukee, where he has a newly remodeled apartment with all the amenities. But he really lives for weekends in ragged blue jeans on his farm and the 100-year-old house he is very slowly restoring. Even the outbuildings are acquiring slate roofs.

He drove us part way to the river in his four-wheel-drive vehicle. Zipping up jackets and pulling on caps, we walked swiftly through wooded bottomland toward the river. The predawn stillness was broken by a raucous flock of crows somewhere upstream. The sound became louder as they approached us. They seemed to resent our intrusion, but after emphatically registering their protest they flew off the other way.

Somewhere in the midst of that invasion we heard the musical gurgling of sandhill cranes. The crows must have told them we were coming; by the time we arrived at the river no cranes were to be seen. The beach, however, was covered with their T-shaped tracks, which made a bold pattern etched in the frosty sand, highlighted by the first light of day. White gulls catching rays of the early sun circled in and out of mists rising from the river, accompanied by the music of their own cries.

Having missed the cranes at sunrise, I decided to try again at sunset. This time we were a group of six, including Jeb Barzen, a wetland ecologist with the International Crane Foundation, and his wife Barb, who postponed celebrating their first wedding anniversary to join us. The others included Matt, his housemate John and our daughter Juliana. Most of us are ONNs, except of course Jeb, an obvious KP.

We arrived well before sunset and settled down at the edge of some trees to wait. A kingfisher tried to entertain us, hovering high above the water and then plummeting suddenly down.

We chatted spasmodically until Jeb said, "Here they come!" I couldn't see them at first, but soon we spotted three flying in, long thin necks outstretched, long thin legs trailing behind. Their sheer size always impresses me — six and a half feet of wingspan in majestic flight. They were almost close enough for us to see their rusty caps.

Six sets of binoculars were trained on the sky. No one moved or made a sound. Seven more sandhills came in, then larger groups. But they didn't stop on the sandbar before us, where Matt had been seeing them. Later Jeb said, "I could tell when they saw us. They flared off."

Occasionally we heard that wonderful wild croaking sound as they tried to decide what to do about these humans who were too close to their resting spot. Some of them circled back, making a beautiful pattern against the full moon rising in the east.

While silently glued to binoculars, I had been counting, and soon found that everyone else had, too. Totals varied from seventy to eighty. About thirty landed on another sandbar and we moved quietly back behind the trees. "Did you see a couple of them do a little dance?" asked Jeb. "They sometimes practice their pair bonding throughout the year."

The cranes' musical croaking continued to scold us. Even though we had moved, they still were restless, so we decided to leave. After we got behind a good screen of trees, we could hear their cries as they circled lower. "They're settling down now," Jeb assured us.

As we headed back to our cars through oak woods, several pairs of great horned owls began to hoot. Jeb explained that the female begins with two notes and then the male chimes in, another example of pair bonding.

"You put on a good show, Matt," we told him as we said goodnight in the gathering darkness. "Peach and gold sunset, pink and blue moonrise, eighty cranes and now a great horned owl."

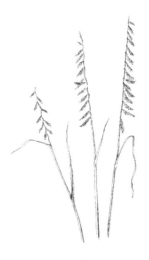

IV.
Beginnings

I always knew that I would become a birder — it was in my genes. My parents knew every bird that came into our yard, even without the aid of binoculars or any really definitive guide book. I grew up in the country, on the shores of Lake Michigan. Norm grew up in Beloit, which wasn't exactly a big city. Both of our families had gardens and our mothers canned most of the fruits and vegetables we ate in winter.

After college, our marriage and Norm's military service in World War II, we settled into Norm's medical practice in Madison and the business of bearing and raising a family. I missed my rural childhood, but during the years of house calls and Saturday office hours, it didn't seem practical to consider living in the country. Our last city home, a five-bedroom, three-bath house, had all the amenities and most labor-saving devices available in 1956. It was our dream house. Built next to a tiny wooded ravine, it helped assuage my longing for the country.

Nevertheless, after our fourth child was born, I began to feel as though my life was bounded by dishes, dusting and diapers. Norm sensed my restlessness and made a suggestion. "You always liked to write. Why don't you go back to it?"

Living in a university town made it easy to take advantage of University Extension writing courses and within a few years I found myself selling feature stories to local papers. The money I earned barely kept me in postage stamps and typing paper but writing was a perfect occupation for me during those busy years. I did stories on everything from a paraplegic who shot a deer to publicity for the local kennel club. Over the next twenty-five years, my articles found homes in five newspapers and about a hundred magazines. It was possible to fit the interviewing and writing time around my home-making and mothering duties. Eventually I realized I preferred writing about travel and nature and limited my work to those subjects.

After we had the cottage a couple of years, I wrote a short article about our bluebird neighbors and took it to Pat Peckham, the editor of our weekly local paper, the *Sauk Prairie Star.* I proposed to do a regular column under the title "From the River Bank." Pat welcomed the idea, as have the two editors who succeeded him.

In the Madison years, if life in a three-generation household, with four children from twos to teens, got too hectic for me, I had one remedy. If I could manage to be somewhere at evening so I could watch the sun setting over a lake, everything was suddenly all right with my world. I was still a country girl at heart, and I dreamed about having a place somewhere on water, preferably one where you could see the sunset reflected in it.

My father lived with us. As far as he was concerned, a proper vacation was spent cooking over an open fire and sleeping in a tent, preferably with a canoe handy. He imbued in all of us a love of outdoor adventures and we took at least two canoe trips annually on the nearby Wisconsin River. Family ski trips to northern Wisconsin (without Grandpa) were as much a part of our year in winter as canoe trips were in summer. When Devil's Head ski area was built about an hour away from Madison, we found we didn't have to drive way up north to ski anymore.

By 1972, when our last child, Juliana, was ready to graduate from high school, Norm decided we should look near Devil's Head for a cottage that we could use both winter and summer. We would then sell the house, which by that time had mostly empty bedrooms, and live in an apartment in the city.

So we found this little, redwood two-bedroom cottage on the Wisconsin River, only forty-five minutes from our Madison home, with twenty-five acres of prairie, woods and bottomland to explore. After two more trips to Devil's head, we never returned to downhill skiing, opting instead for cross-country skiing out our front door.

Those were the Vietnam War years, and *Endlichheim,* as we called it, was our oasis. To my immense joy, the summer sun set over the river.

Only our oldest daughter, Karen, followed traditional patterns. She was "pinned" in her sophomore year, engaged in her junior year and married in her senior year of college. By the time we bought the cottage, she already had moved to Anchorage, Alaska with her schoolteacher husband, Tom, and produced a cherished grandson for us.

Her brother, Curt, only two years younger, was caught up in the Vietnam War dilemma. He decided to live the simple life in Canada with the puzzled and concerned support of his parents. Eventually he was able to return to the U.S. but continued for some time to live the "hippie" life. Kristin and Juliana also were profoundly affected by the turmoil of the times. By turns in and out of college, they spurned most of the creature comforts they had grown up with.

Norm's Friday afternoons were free, so the two of us would spend weekends at the river, as family and friends soon came to refer to our new acreage. It was a short drive for Norm to return to the city for Saturday morning office hours. At first, we kept the gate to our long driveway locked when we were away. On arrival, I would get out and unlock the gate and tell Norm, "You drive in. I'm going to walk."

During the summer months, as I enjoyed a leisurely stroll to the house and river, I was usually accompanied by the musical trill of a field sparrow singing somewhere in the middle of the meadow. As his notes ran gradually from loud to soft, I could feel tension running out of my spine. On Monday morning we returned to face our challenges. We learned much from our puzzling children.

Norm and I spent every weekend exploring our new kingdom, making few changes except to try to re-establish some of the prairie grasses and flowers that once grew here. It never ceases to amaze us that the more we learn, the more there is to learn about the natural world. We had been birders ever since moving to the big house and were thrilled as we began to get acquainted with our avian neighbors.

One of our first purchases after we bought the cottage was, of course, a bird feeder. "Go see Henry Koenig," helpful neighbors suggested. "His wife Edna is the bird lady."

In their beautiful old Victorian house in Sauk City, they took care of the many injured birds people brought them. Already in their sixties, they devoted all their time to this task. They seldom went anywhere, because the work was so demanding; but they never were lonely because the world beat a path to their door. In certain rooms, separated by hanging screens, birds were allowed to fly free. Paper toweling covered every inch of table tops to catch the droppings. The place was spotless.

We purchased one of the squirrel-proof, all-metal feeders that Henry designed and built. We went home and installed it but no

To Thank a River

birds came. We could see a cardinal every time we went for a walk in the woods, but the level of sunflower seed in the feeder just didn't go down. Our "Swiss daughter" Marianne was an exchange student who lived with us that year. "In Switzerland, we put some leaves and things around the feeder. Maybe if you do that, they will come," she said.

We easily found some white pine boughs, which Marianne arranged around the base of the feeder. Eventually one pair of cardinals began coming, as well as the goldfinches and juncos we were familiar with in the city. Twenty years later we can scarcely look out our four riverfront windows in winter without seeing a pair of cardinals and several juncos and chickadees.

Debating whether to make the cottage our permanent home, we spent the winter of 1975 living at the river and Norm commuted to Madison. As Norm put it, "We wanted to see if the getaway part would go away, but the longer we stayed here, the more we knew we wanted to live here."

Those were the early years of the oil crisis and we were very concerned about what the consumer-oriented lifestyle of our contemporaries was doing to the environment. When we decided to remodel the cottage, we eschewed most of the luxuries of our big house in the city and didn't miss them at all. We had added a large screened porch in 1973 to the north side of the cottage and a few years later we built a sun room on the south side. But we still have only two bedrooms and one bathroom. Our motor home serves as a guest house when needed.

Harold Buehlow from neighboring Mazomanie was the carpenter who turned our cottage into a home. We moved in early because I wanted to be on hand for decisions as they came up, and so Norm could help with things like staining the woodwork. Harold put up with our presence as he carefully carried out the plans we had sketched for him. I remember the thrill I felt in April 1976 when Norm installed at the end of our driveway the rural mailbox that said CLAUSEN 9928.

When Kristin was studying at the university, she persuaded me to audit an ornithology class with her. I'll always be grateful to her for insisting, even though that was the spring we were remodeling the cottage and I didn't think I could spare the time. She and I still enjoy birding as well as keying out new flowers and plants together.

She and Juliana eventually finished their education and found good jobs. We enjoy their company and their friends immensely and are grateful that both live nearby. If any heavy work is to be done, the girls come to help and bring strong young men. Juliana and Richard eventually moved to a house only two miles down the river, so we call on them frequently.

Our hippie son now has an MBA, a wife, three children and a mortgage. He is a vice president of the largest bank in Seattle. Karen and Tom now have four children. When all of them visit at one time, some of them bring tents. Family reunions tend to occur in summer. All four of our children seem to consider our river place as home, even though they didn't grow up here.

V.
Sounds of spring

"There's one of those springs sparrows that migrate through," said Norm one morning in early April. "The ones with black and white stripes on the head."

A bird guide and binoculars (both his and mine) are always handy on the table in front of the windows where we eat breakfast and lunch. After checking the sparrows, we knew we had to be looking at either a white-throated or white-crowned sparrow. Soon the bird raised his head so I could see the white throat.

"Old Sam Peabody, Peabody, Peabody!" That's what the white-throated sparrow's song is supposed to sound like. It is definite, spirited and vigorous in spring: a wavering echo of itself in fall.

"Old Sam" passes through here on the way to and from nesting grounds north of the border. It is one of the most common birds on Isle Royale in Lake Superior not far from Canada.

This fellow scratches like a chicken, while house sparrows (a different species) are not quite so zealous in their search for food. They take what they can spot on the surface.

Some time later I thought I had discovered an unusual bird. It looked like a white-throated sparrow, but had a tiny yellow spot between its eye and bill, which was not noticeable except through binoculars. I had seen hundreds of white-throated sparrows before, and never noticed that. So I began paging through my bird guide. Sure enough, there's a bird with black and white crown stripes and those yellow spots. And it was — a white-throated sparrow. I guess you can always learn something new about an old friend.

❧❧❧

Music seems to come from every oak tree these spring days, but there are no hidden loudspeakers. It is the genuine article. About the first of May it is mostly brown thrasher songs. We look forward each spring with pleasure to the return of this bird; it's the most music we've heard from one bird voice for many months. Not only are his notes beautiful and varied; he sings each one twice so he's sure we'll understand.

Early in May the Baltimore oriole arrives, or rather several of them. They are all singing to try to establish a nesting territory. The song sparrow joins the chorus, forming a lovely chamber music ensemble.

Soon they are joined by several wrens. For a small bird, wrens surely produce a volume and variety. On Mother's Day, I often hear another song: equally melodious, but more liquid, a long varied tune, usually from the top of an oak. The rose-breasted grosbeak has returned, as a special favor for bird-watching mothers.

Next the catbird shows up. His song could be mistaken for that of a brown thrasher, since both tend to mimic other birds. However, the catbird doesn't say everything twice, and he also inserts a *meow* every now and then to clearly establish his identity. Finally we have a full symphony, going on at intervals all day long.

When Kristin and I took our ornithology class, Jed Burtt led our quiz sections and field trips. Although he was not very tall, we all looked up to him because of his infinite knowledge of birds and for his gentle, genial personality. He told us that although bird songs and calls may sound identical to most humans, actually they have individual variations with meaning for other birds. These sounds enable mates, parents and offspring to recognize each other. The social functions of bird songs and calls include synchronizing flights, such as in migration. How else could a hundred grackles decide to leave simultaneously for the South?

Birds are good at passing along information to each other, too. Surely each bird doesn't have to find out for himself that the neighbor's big orange cat is lurking near my feeder. And there must be some explanation for the fact that dozens of goldfinches appeared out of nowhere the morning after our friends put out a new thistle feeder.

❧❧❧

Early one morning in late May I went walking with two ONNs, Juliana and Richard's sister, Deborah. We had the privilege of being

To Thank a River 43

accompanied by Becky Isenring, definitely a KP. In addition to being a wife and mother of two, she was working on her second college career, a degree in wildlife ecology. In her first college years, when she and Deborah were close friends, she studied the French horn. Her keen musical ear enables her to recognize most birds by song alone.

If possible, I always join a KP on a bird walk. It helps to know what bird we're looking for, and whether we should be searching on the ground or how far up in the trees.

We started out through the thick woods of the Mazomanie bottomlands. Leaves that were almost full size concealed a veritable symphony of singers. Rose-breasted grosbeaks, orioles, indigo buntings, vireos, yellowthroats — I could recognize some of these songs but Becky knew them all. We had especially good views of the scarlet tanager and the indigo bunting. I've seen both occasionally near our house, but for nesting they prefer deep woods.

Our trail led us on to the comparative brightness of the dike road, along a channel of open water on our left. Beyond this was a large marsh with small trees and bushes along its near margin. Far across the marsh, we saw and heard great blue herons and sandhill cranes. Eventually, the loud distress call of two Canada geese told us in no uncertain terms that we were too close to their nest. "We'd better head back and leave them alone," suggested Juliana. "We've been walking for over an hour anyway."

As we walked back along the dike road, we passed within ten feet of a yellow warbler pulling nesting material from dried grasses. A loud *witchety witchety witch* directed us to a tree just across the water. His black mask was in sharp contrast to his bright yellow body, and he is simply called a yellowthroat.

"There's a northern water thrush," said Becky, pointing to some brush at the edge of the marsh. He moved into plain sight so we could all get a good look at the striped breast and yellow eye stripe. Looking at my bird guide, I asked how she could distinguish so quickly between the northern and Louisiana water thrush. "The Louisiana has a very white eye stripe," she said.

Then we got into vireos, which are even harder to sort out. The warbling, the red-eyed and the Philadelphia all sing from tree tops but manage to keep their nondescript gray selves pretty well concealed. So we had a short lesson in vireos. The warbling vireo warbles on endlessly; the red-eyed speaks in short robin-like phrases. The Philadelphia's song is similar to that of the red-eyed, but higher pitched and slower. If you can see him, you can distinguish him from the red-eyed because he has a yellow breast. The other two have white breasts.

The next day I was leading a group of fourth graders on a nature trail, when the teacher who accompanied them asked me what that yellow bird was up there. "Could be a yellow warbler," I suggested. "No, it's bigger than a warbler," he replied.

I could see the yellow breast and gray back, and said, "If it would sing I could probably tell you what it is." It promptly sang several robin-like phrases. "Philadelphia vireo!" I announced, thanks to my tutor of the day before.

❋❋❋

I remember Jed saying in ornithology class: "If you really want to learn to identify warblers you should learn their songs."

My memory for bird songs is not very reliable when I hear them all summer. How would I ever learn songs for those I hear only a short time in spring? But I tried.

One May day a few years later I found that it really works. On a field trip to Baxter's Hollow with a naturalist from the University of Wisconsin-Baraboo, our KP tossed out the remark, "There's a blue-winged warbler. I don't see him, but you can hear him. He sounds like an insect."

Gradually I learned to distinguish his voice — a two-level buzz with the first z-z-z on a higher note. The next day in the river bottoms near Mazomanie we heard the same buzzing.

We were a smaller group this time, neighbors who used to hike together every Tuesday morning in May. "I think that's the blue-winged warbler I heard yesterday," I told them. "Hear that buzzing sound?"

We all stood like statues, binoculars aimed about halfway up in oak trees, where the sound seemed to be coming from. Other warbler sounds were heard, but the tiny singers were elusive. Oak leaves fortunately were not full size and couldn't hide warblers forever. The leaves were like Japanese tracery against a blue and white sky.

When we caught sight of movement with the naked eye we raised our binoculars quickly. With a little luck we got a few details of color or markings before our quarry hid again. "He's mostly yellow," reported Caroline Plank.

"I see white wing bars," said Mary Muessel.

The next time we saw him he flew to another tree and lifted his tiny pointed beak to pour forth his signature buzzing. Yes, the wings and tail were blue-gray, just like the blue-wing pictured in the guide. Knowing the song ahead of time made it considerably easier to find him among the forty-some listed warbler species.

We read that he often feeds in lower branches and in bushes and that his nest is built on or near the ground in dense vegetation. He breeds in southern Wisconsin and likes streams or swamp margins.

This explains why we saw him along Otter Creek and also in the Wisconsin River bottoms. Since then I try to remember that all sibilant sounds heard in the woods are not made by insects.

✲✲✲

"Look at that grackle," said Kristin one May afternoon as we were sipping tea at the table by the window. The grackle was parading around with his iridescent blue-green head pointing at the sky. About this time of year birds use body language as well as song to communicate with each other. Sometimes two of them will face each other and strut around in a pattern. Even an ordinary house sparrow looks impressive as it swaggers about on a limb of the cherry tree.

These birds are, of course, trying to attract a mate. If there is a female participating, she is either accepting or rejecting his proposal.

"A simple yes or no doesn't usually happen in the animal world," a KP told us one time.

The female often looks over several males to decide which has the most desirable characteristics to hand down to future generations — part of nature's plan for the survival of the fittest. Another ritual that birds often go through in spring is the feeding of the female by the male. She does most of her own food-gathering, but when he finds a special tidbit, he will offer it to her. By accepting it, she says, "You'll make a good provider; we'll raise a family."

Birds who later share incubation duties sometimes indicate by posturing when it is time to change places on the nest. Birds use belligerent postures to chase off rivals. In early spring our ornithology class went to a marsh to observe male redwing blackbirds defending their territory. If another male encroached, feathers rose, wings spread and the familiar *honk-a-ree* took on a more strident tone. Then we could see the yellow epaulets above the male's red shoulders, which are not ordinarily visible.

I remember a very cold day in late winter when Jed took us to the Yahara River to watch mallards show off their mating postures. We were supposed to watch for the tail-shake, head-flick, bill-shake, grunt-whistle, head up, tail up, nod-swimming, turning back of head. "I can't quite see all that," I confessed when Jed wandered by.

"They're performing most of the postures," he assured me.

In addition to all that, I read somewhere that the female may take an "inciting posture," a lowering and pointing of the head, when she sees an enemy which she wants her mate to attack. Being a bird is certainly more complicated than I thought.

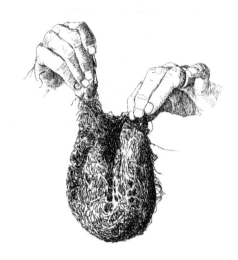

VI.
Birds of Summer

We hadn't lived here very long when, about mid-May, a melodic, whistled song kept calling me away from my morning chores. It alternated with a single slurred note, equally melodic, that kept saying to me: *C'mere. C'mere.*

This was an invitation I could not resist. With dishes in the sink and beds unmade, I took binoculars in hand and went out to try to find this newly arrived bird. He was elusive and stayed high in the tops of oaks, but a flash of brilliant orange as he flew to another tree was finally my reward — the northern oriole.

Each summer since then we have enjoyed the beautiful contrast of his bright-orange breast and rump with black hood, wings and tail. I had never noticed how frequently a brilliantly colored bird will have black wings until Jed pointed it out in ornithology class. He said that melamine in the coloration of the feathers, which makes them black, also makes them more durable. Since flight feathers are so crucial to the survival of a bird, durability is vital.

"We found the oriole's nest," announced the note we found one day a year or so later as we returned from an extended trip. The message was from Connie and Pat Peckham who often house-sat for us in those early years.

I immediately called Pat at his office for directions. "The nest is so obvious, once you've spotted it," he told me. "In an oak tree, almost at the end of a branch that points toward the river. You can see it right from your living room windows."

I stood inside the house and looked with binoculars, combing every branch of several different trees. Finally I wandered outside, looking up in the trees from different angles, but I saw nothing that looked like a nest. Both male and female orioles were flying about, saying *C'mere,* probably telling each other where the best insects were.

I finally settled in a chair in the shade of a big oak near the house and read again about the intricate nest the female weaves, firmly anchoring it at the top to some twigs so it swings safely in any breeze. She uses plant fibers, hair, yarn or string and lines it with the softer fibers. This may take her as much as a week and the nest is used for only one brood and one season. She may return to the same tree again but will build a new nest.

I also read that early colonists noted that this bright orange bird with black head and wings wore the family colors of the Lords Baltimore, who colonized Maryland. They called him the Baltimore bird and he was known as the Baltimore oriole. At one time the powers that be changed it to the northern oriole, but I understand they have changed their minds again — just when I had succeeded in breaking myself of the habit of saying "Baltimore oriole." The female's colors are similar to those of the male, but more subtle — olive green, brown and pale orange.

Eventually I saw our female fly to the lowest branch of the oak I was sitting under. She slipped in behind some leaves near the end of the branch, perhaps twenty feet off the ground. Beneath the leaves, in plain sight as I had been told, was the bottom of a typical hanging basket oriole's nest. The leaves completely concealed the top of the nest and the mother bird.

She stayed about long enough to lay an egg. For a couple of weeks, we saw only the male. Mother does the incubating, while father feeds her and fights off intruders. We saw him threaten a blue jay that got too close one day.

After I had located the nest, I couldn't go by the window or the tree outside without seeing it. The nest is obvious, all right, but the bird herself had to show it to me.

One day during a storm, very high winds tossed that nest as much as three feet back and forth. Trying to follow the motion with binoculars made me dizzy. Undoubtedly the mother was sitting on the nest, but I couldn't be sure because of the protective covering of leaves and the depth of the nest. That little branch was exposed to the strongest winds coming up the river and I wondered aloud, "Why did she choose such a vulnerable spot?"

"Well, not many predators could come that far out on the limb," Norm pointed out. "Closer to the tree, where the limbs are stronger, the nest would be in full view."

"That's true," I agreed. "The heaviest concentration of leaves seems to be out at the ends of branches."

After about two weeks, which is normal incubation time, we saw the mother bird fly in with a tidbit in her mouth. She didn't stay long and immediately the father came in with his contribution. After delivering the insect, he reappeared on the limb above, looking down uncertainly. He uttered a few notes, then looked again in every direction. The song became more imperious, the searching appeared more frantic. Only when he saw the mother returning did he leave his post.

Perhaps he was a first-time father and didn't know what to do about these suddenly hungry creatures. "Where are you, Mother? I can't leave these children here alone!" (Kristin's interpretation.)

For two weeks the oriole parents worked from dawn to dusk to feed their young. Sometimes we heard high-pitched little squeaks coming from the nest every time a parent flew near. It sounded as though they were saying, *Feed-me-me-me.*

Once when I was standing beneath the tree and father flew in with an insect in his beak, he settled on a branch several feet away and looked at me. Rather than go to the young bird, he flew off to another tree. In spite of pleading from the young ones, he didn't return to feed until I went into the house.

A veritable supermarket stands just a few feet from the nest — a mulberry tree with ripening berries. We would look up from the breakfast table and see not only orioles but catbirds, robins and rose-breasted grosbeaks taking home supplies for their young.

Eventually we heard a deeper, more adolescent voice from the oriole nest with an identical reply from somewhere in an oak beyond the sheds. Father was still in attendance but mother was nowhere to be seen. We concluded that she was in charge of fledglings already out of the nest.

Next morning the last reluctant baby made it to a branch below the nest, where he still chirped expectantly every time father appeared with food. The young bird seemed to have an insatiable appetite and I wondered how mother was coping off in the woods somewhere if there were two or three for her to feed and protect, since orioles typically lay four eggs.

The chubby baby on the branch looked about half the size of the father, possessing a very short tail. His fuzzy breast was speckled with orange and when he was pleading for food he fluttered his wings, plainly showing the black and white wing pattern.

I wondered how long the young bird would sit on the limb. Would he hop back into the nest at night? In spite of the drama being presented before me, I couldn't watch all day. Duties called me away from the window. About 11 a.m., I looked up to see the branch empty; I saw neither father nor child again that day.

Presumably the family was reunited somewhere in the thick underbrush that covers most of our riverbank. Two days later, on a scorching hot day, we saw a baby oriole hop along the ground, several feet from the protective underbrush. We watched him reach the shade of a young oak, then we departed, presuming that a parent would come and coax him back to safety. This must be a stressful time for avian parents, trying to control, protect and feed several adolescents who are eager to explore their world but not really prepared to cope. And we thought raising human adolescents was a challenge.

❧❧❧

"You've got bluebirds feeding young in that tree," said one of our first visitors, almost spilling his iced tea as he gestured toward the fallen tree not thirty feet from our living room windows. Since we were still in our weekend phase, we had missed that little phenomenon, although we were always thrilled to see and hear this now rare bird. A few weeks later, one sunny afternoon, bluebirds seemed to be teaching their young to fly by cascading off our roof onto that same fallen tree.

The next year we were more observant. We watched them build a nest in a hole in an upright branch of that same tree. Often the male would sing on a branch above while the female carried wisps of grass into the hole. His song is a soft, delicate one and if you couldn't see his beak moving, you would think the singer was in a distant tree. I'm told he says *cheer cheerful charmer* — a catchword that is quite helpful in recognizing the song.

By the end of May the male and female were taking turns at the nest, feeding young. As they worked in the morning sun, we admired the intense blue of the male's back, nicely relieved by pale underparts and a rusty red breast. The female is more gray than blue, but there is enough color in her wings and tail to provide a respectable flash of blue when she flies.

"Can you believe how brave those little bluebirds are against bigger birds?" I commented one day. If a redheaded woodpecker lit on the fallen tree, the male bluebird made determined passes close over his head, with a menacing-looking open beak. Sometimes it was a bluejay that had the menacing open beak while both bluebird parents flew wildly back and forth in a big arc, with the jay at its lowest point. The large birds always gave up and the bluebirds never did.

After a couple of years, the log began to decay, the roof leaked and we missed having the bluebirds for such close neighbors. We put up several proper bluebird boxes, two within sight of the house. One is usually occupied by tree swallows (also delightful neighbors) and the other by a pair of bluebirds, but neither box is near enough for such close scrutiny.

❧❧❧

Friendly, noisy, aggressive, feisty, a beautiful singer — all these descriptions have been applied to the same bird, the house wren. He has also been labeled nefarious — wicked or vicious — and I'm afraid that's true.

It's not hard to tell the arrival date of the wren. He lets the world know at once with his burst of rapid-fire song. Only about four inches long, he has a reddish brown back with faint darker barring and a long tail that sometimes sticks straight up in the air. Chippewa Indians gave him a long name meaning "a big noise for its size." He has a sharp needle-like bill and is known for occasionally breaking the eggs or killing the young in the nests of other birds.

One evening we were having supper on the porch with our friends Sally and Joe Benforado when we heard loud distress calls coming from a nesting box occupied by a pair of wrens. A redheaded woodpecker was determinedly pulling out every stick of the wrens' nest and throwing it on the ground, all the while subject to attack by the ousted pair. The woodpecker finally turned around and jabbed at a wren, apparently impaling a wing. He flew off across the meadow carrying the loudly protesting wren. The distraught mate followed, uttering his own distress calls.

At this point Sally decided she needed something from the kitchen and I called to her: "You're missing all the excitement."

"I just didn't want to watch anymore," she said. She did return, though, in time to see the woodpecker come back. While he finished the nest-wrecking job in a systematic manner, both wrens sat quietly on another branch — watching. The impaled wren had evidently been unhurt but had learned a lesson. If we weren't aware of the wren's nefarious reputation, our sympathies would have all been with that tiny little bird attacked by that big bully of a woodpecker.

❧❧❧

"Bobolink! Bobolink! Bobolink! Spink, spank, spink!" I said as Juliana, Richard and I walked through the tall grass field. "Is that what you hear?" asked Richard.

We were listening to the songs of a bird I hadn't seen in years and

To Thank a River

that was a line from a poem I once memorized at the country school of my childhood in Kenosha County. I thought it a pretty good description of the bubbling notes that had a sort of metallic quality to them — even though my companions did not quite agree.

Male bobolinks arrive early in May from wintering grounds in South America. They settle into hayfields to select and loudly guard a small territory that looks as though it will have plenty of insects. When the females come they are actively pursued, as the mating seems to depend on ladies' choice. When they have made up their minds, the females use last year's dried materials to form a flimsy nest, well hidden at the base of a clump of tall grass. Then both parents set about raising their brood of five to seven young.

Richard and a friend, R.K., explored this hayfield in May, listening carefully to the songs of individual birds. "We counted twenty different males and we could distinguish individual territories because the birds stopped singing as soon as they flew over someone else's territory," Richard told us.

With special equipment, they taped fourteen of the songs, each with its own minor but distinctive differences. R.K. knew that someone from the UW-Madison had done a study on bobolinks here twenty years earlier and he looked up the resulting thesis. It turns out that the research had been done on this very field. Apparently the descendants of those birds are still coming to raise their young here.

As we walked through the field in June, the singing was less obvious. The birds were too busy feeding young. Male bobolinks are unique in appearance — the only ones I know with black breasts and large white patches on back and wings. The back of the male's head is a buffy yellow. The female is slightly smaller. With dark brown stripes on the head and a finch-type bill, she looks like a sparrow. Bobolinks belong to a family of icterids — blackbirds and orioles — and they do have heavy bills. But most of the other icterids have longer bills that don't look so finch-like.

My reference book contains the following note on bobolinks: "Early cutting of hay and grain (before July 15) is its worst hazard and its abundance is largely dependent on local mowing dates." We hoped the local mower would wait.

VII.
More about birds

"Are you the lady that writes the column about birds?" an urgent voice on the phone asked one July day. "I've got baby owls on a branch right outside my kitchen window. I can't believe it. Someone ought to come and take a picture." The voice belonged to Kathy Thimling of Sauk City.

I quickly gathered bird book, camera and Peter, my visiting grandson with especially sharp eyes, and headed for the address she gave me. "I hope they'll still be here," Kathy had said as we hung up.

They were, huddled together along the limb of a big old apple tree not thirty feet from her kitchen sink. We went quietly out the back door and stood right under them. Their limb was eight or ten feet above my head. Three were snuggled together, the fourth a few inches away.

"Five were flying around here last night, but now there are only four," said Kathy. While I took some pictures with a flash to penetrate their leafy domain, Kathy and Peter searched this tree and another nearby to look for number five.

"There's the fifth one!" Peter finally said. It was staring down impassively at us from a high branch.

We began wondering about the parents. Because the young had ear tufts, I knew they had to be either screech or great horned owls. They seemed almost as large already as screech owls, but they were all gray. Owls hatch in early spring, so they would be nearly full-grown by this time.

"There's another gray one, farther up and closer to the trunk," called out Peter. "And there's the mother, way up near the top!"

She was a rusty red screech owl. The color problem was cleared up by checking the bird book. Screech owls can be either gray or red. Often a red and gray will mate and this seemed to have been the case here. The Thimlings reported seeing them every day for the rest of the week, always with a gray or red adult in attendance.

"The young didn't pay any attention to us," Kathy reported. "But one adult — usually the gray one — followed us constantly with her eyes. We could tell the difference not only by size, but the adults had much larger talons. Their ear tufts looked bigger, too."

One afternoon three of the owlets took baths in the bird bath, drying out on a platform just outside the kitchen window. "If the screen hadn't been there, I could have touched them," Kathy told us.

Screech owls have become suburban birds. They nest in cavities in trees, sometimes old hawk or flicker nests, close to open areas where they can find mice, shrews, snakes or sparrows for food.

Owls hunt at night, depending on their keen hearing to locate prey. Their feathers are constructed so they fly silently, increasing their chances of surprising the object of their search. When first hatched in April, screech owls are quite helpless. At that time the parents don't hesitate to attack anything, human or otherwise, that approaches the nest too closely. I reported this bit of information to Kathy, who replied:

"We've had lots of people in and out of our yard to see these owls. I guess we're lucky we didn't get bombarded."

❧❧❧

In midsummer, bird songs and calls sound a little different. They seem more insistent and sometimes more discordant. Some of these sounds come from parent birds teaching their offspring about life on the outside and some come from the young birds begging for attention and food.

House sparrows are not my favorite birds but even they look appealing when the adult offers a tidbit to the overgrown chick following her. The young are as large as the parents by now and sometimes it is hard to be sure which is which. In general, the young fly more awkwardly and their feathers are apt to look rather unkempt. When hungry, they spread their wings slightly and do a little shimmy, accompanied by a plaintive call. If the immatures have different plumage, it's difficult to match them up unless you see them being fed.

Even that doesn't always work. "Look at that odd-looking couple," said a surprised Juliana one August afternoon.

A chipping sparrow was hopping about the grass industriously plucking seeds and small insects. His rusty cap, neat plumage and smaller size easily sets him apart from the house sparrow. He was shadowed by a much larger bird of nondescript gray color, noisily begging for food and insistently following the chipping sparrow's every move. He was frequently rewarded with a morsel of food.

"Look in the bird guide and see what a baby cowbird looks like," I suggested. "They don't raise their own young. They just deposit an egg in any handy nest and go on their merry way." That's what it was all right, an immature cowbird.

"I wonder what happened to the chipping sparrow young," Juliana mused.

"That's the sad part," I said. "The cowbird either hatches first or is so much bigger and stronger that the host bird's own chicks don't have a chance."

"Everything doesn't always fit together neatly in nature, does it?" she concluded.

❧❧❧

"That must be a cardinal, but where is his crest?" remarked Norm one morning in late summer. We are accustomed to admiring the beauty and perfection of certain birds that we see almost daily. When they go through their molting period, we either mourn right along with them or we laugh because they look so ridiculous.

Feathers are missing in places; one about to come out may be off at an odd angle; the bird looks discolored in spots. A molting bird is not pretty. This period is also hard on him physically. The energy requirements of a molting bird go up twenty-five percent; he needs to eat a lot of protein, as that's what feathers are largely composed of.

Feathers in good condition are crucial to a bird's survival. They are light, flexible structures, therefore they are not durable and take a great deal of care. The bird you see sitting in the sun and grooming himself is not being vain. It's a life and death matter. The feathers have to be zipped up and put back in place regularly. If you ever pulled a chicken feather in the wrong direction and then zipped it back up again, you can understand what he's doing. If everything isn't in place, a bird can't fly.

Even with the best of care, the feathers eventually wear out and must be replaced once or twice a year. This process may appear to be haphazard, but it happens in a certain order, beginning in the center of the feather tracts and moving outward. Some of our bird friends don't show up at all while molting. The process seems to have a psychological as well as a physical effect on them. They become silent, cryptic in their actions, avoid long flight and rest a lot.

Molting occurs at different times with different species. It must occur at the optimum time as far as food supply goes. Other demands on the birds' energy must be avoided, such as winter and, of course, the periods of breeding, nesting and migration.

"There's a pair of cardinals feeding two young," Norm observed one evening at dusk. "They must be from a late nesting — the adults have begun to molt!" Young cardinals resemble the female but have dark beaks. One of the young had so much red in his plumage that we assumed him to be a male. The mother was stuffing sunflower seeds into his throat, while the father did the same for the less colorful chick.

Next day one of the young birds was feeding himself quite competently. Something strange was going on with two of the others. Father seemed to be chasing another bird away from himself, but they flew so fast we couldn't be sure who it was. It may have been the young one, still begging.

Kristin watched a while and remarked that feeding young and molting simultaneously would be difficult. "I can just hear him: 'Gladys, we've got to get these kids weaned. I just don't have enough energy.'"

❦❦❦

One winter day, Juliana, Kristin and I were having lunch in front of the windows when we noticed a small hawk fly into the cherry tree. It didn't stay long and we had quite a discussion afterward as to its identity.

The hooked beak and upright posture established it as a hawk of some kind and we all agreed it had a gray back. I remembered a light breast and striped tail. Kristin saw a rusty breast and didn't see the tail. Juliana was sure it was a merlin, which was a first for her.

I thought I had seen a merlin here in winter several years ago, but was told by a KP that they don't stay here the year round. "It was probably a sharp-shinned hawk," he concluded.

I checked my bird guide and saw how easily the mistake could be made. To me it seems odd that in the text there are several clues as to how to distinguish a sharp-shinned from a Cooper's hawk, but no comparison with the merlin. There is an explanation, but not so logical from the amateur point of view. An experienced birder knows the difference between a falcon and an accipiter, both of which are hawks. But you have to see them in flight. Falcons (which a merlin is) have narrow, pointed wings and accipiters (the sharp-shinned) have broad, rounded wings. This time we didn't get a good look at our hawk in flight.

56 Clausen

A few days later I glanced out the window and saw a small hawk perched in an ash tree. This time I memorized the field marks. It was clearly a sharp-shinned: gray back, dark head, horizontal rusty breast stripes and a striped tail.

Sharp-shinned hawks nest in northern Wisconsin and on up into Canada and Alaska, spending the winter from this area down into the Gulf states and Mexico. They are said to prey upon birds as large as pigeons. My visitor looked innocent enough, but I noticed no small birds were in sight as long as he stayed.

People often ask me what I do about hawks in my bird-feeding area. I don't *do* anything except enjoy them. You don't often see them catch anything. Besides, they also eat rodents. As Ken Lange, the naturalist, puts it: "A hawk dining on a song bird is a fact of nature, a dramatic event in the food chain."

❧❧❧

Have you ever stopped to wonder why a bird can fly? After hearing a lecture on the subject by a professor of ornithology, I'm still not sure I know why, but I did learn a lot of interesting facts.

Thousands of golden plovers fly 2,500 miles from the Aleutian Islands in Alaska to the Hawaiian Islands with no opportunity to feed en route. How do they survive? We get a clue from some information about gulls in flight.

A gull uses 0.015 percent of its weight to fly one kilometer. Many birds can store fat amounting to twenty-five or fifty percent of their weight so, at that rate, gulls could fly more than a thousand kilometers without seriously depleting their body weight.

Another fascinating bit: a flying bird is twenty-five to fifty percent more efficient in energy consumption per kilometer traveled than a walking or running mammal of the same size.

Since early in this century, humans have managed to apply some of the principles that enable a bird to fly and produced flying machines. But human results are not only much noisier, they are less efficient in energy consumption per kilometer traveled.

It is clean aerodynamic design that allows a bird to pass through the air smoothly with little friction and a high degree of stability. The vital organs and heaviest muscles are placed between and beneath the wings. This helps to provide automatic stability requiring little muscular correction.

As birds evolved from early ancestors, they developed weight-reducing and power-increasing adaptions that gave them all the efficiency we have been talking about. Some examples: thin, hollow bones made strong with struts inside them; elimination of teeth and heavy jaws; feathers instead of fur for insulators; a diet of concentrated energy-rich food with rapid and efficient digestion; high glucose content of blood; a four-chambered heart which provides double circulation; a highly efficient respiratory system; and several other adaptations which were a little too technical for me.

So I still don't really understand those aerodynamic principles that allow planes and birds to fly. But I am now more impressed when I watch the ballet of the gulls or the powerful, purposeful flight of an eagle.

❧❧❧

"If you go into town today, you'd better get some more suet at the locker plant," Norm reminds me every few weeks during the winter months. "Our woodpeckers need it." Downy, hairy and red-bellied woodpeckers are our regular customers.

I wish I had a nickel for every time a visitor has said, "There's a redheaded woodpecker." I also wish I could *see* a redheaded woodpecker once in a while. Twenty years ago, we saw them often but no more. I have to tell the aforementioned visitor that what he is looking at is a red-bellied woodpecker. The bird does have a pale orange spot on his belly, but his most prominent feature is a satiny red hood; his back is horizontally striped black and white. Downies and hairies have plain white backs, white bellies and are mostly black elsewhere with some white in the wings. The males have a small red spot at the back of the head.

"Is that a downy or a hairy? It looks too big for a downy," said my friend Sara one winter afternoon over a cup of tea by the window.

"I finally learned the best way to tell them apart," I told her. "Check the bill. If it's almost as long as his head, it's a hairy."

Usually the hairy woodpecker is about two inches longer than the downy, but we have seen big downies and small hairies. The hairy has, besides that extremely large, strong bill, a tongue twice as long as his head, incredible as that may seem. That tongue can draw larvae of destructive beetle grubs out of a tree, which is his gain as well as that of the tree.

A woodpecker's bill is designed for drilling deep into trees, preferably dead ones, for insects and their larvae, as well as for digging nest cavities. They drill deep into a tree each spring to excavate new nest holes, ten to twelve inches deep in the case of hairies and downies. They lay four or five white eggs on the wood chips that collect on the bottom. Mates share the tasks of nest-building and brooding. The male usually takes the night shift; perhaps he feels better equipped to guard against the possibility of a marauding raccoon. It is fortunate that woodpeckers feel the urge to dig out a new nesting site each year; the holes are subsequently used by nuthatches, chickadees or even flying squirrels, all of which are ill-equipped to dig their own. Just another example of how interdependent all living creatures are. And that includes humans.

❦❦❦

If the king of our river is the eagle, the king of our river bottomlands must be the pileated woodpecker. They are shy birds, though, and clever at concealing themselves in the more densely wooded areas.

We've been fortunate enough to have them visit several times. I once enthusiastically reported a sighting to Sally Benforado on the telephone when she asked what they looked like. "Like a giant red-headed woodpecker, only triangular," I replied.

"Triangular?" she asked. I really couldn't tell her what I meant by that.

Soon after I learned that Henry and Edna Koenig were caring for a pileated woodpecker at their bird hospital in Sauk City. Norm and I went to get better acquainted with the species. Their visits to our place have been too fleeting for adequate observation. My impression had usually been of a big awkward chicken with a red head who perched momentarily on a tree but found it not to his liking and flew away.

The Koenig's guest had been found stunned near Gannon's Resort and brought to them several days before. They put her in the biggest cage they had. They told us she just sat disconsolately on the floor at first and was injuring delicate feathers on the wire sides.

So Henry built a bigger cage, about three-by-four-by-four feet, lining the lower part with plastic to protect the feathers which would be so important when she flew again. "I think she must miss her tree trunk to perch on," said Edna.

"Why don't I bring in a log from our wood pile?" Norm said. "Maybe she would perch on that."

Babe, as they called her at Gannon's, was delighted when this addition to her quarters arrived. She clambered over to the log immediately, clamping her big scrawny feet like wires to the bark. After that she came down only for the crickets and bugs Edna fed her. She even slept up on the log.

Babe pecked away so industriously at her stump that a pile of chips an inch deep had sometimes accumulated by the end of the day. Occasionally Henry took her out and held her by the legs to get her to try her wings. As soon as the weather moderated and she was strong enough, they released her in the same woods where she had been found.

Pileated woodpeckers remain in the same territory the year-round

To Thank a River 59

and it takes a large wooded area to support one pair. Carpenter ants are their favorite food and they dig oblong holes in dead or live trees to find the ant colony hiding behind the bark.

Their nest hole is apt to be found high in a dead tree. It leads to a cylindrical chamber fifteen to twenty-four inches deep, with the opening about four inches across. Each year the pileated parents make a new home for their one annual brood, although the nest is always in the same area or may even be in the same tree. Old holes are often used by owls, flying squirrels or wood ducks.

We could tell Babe was a female because she had a black forehead. The male's forehead would be red like the crest. The angle of her crest and long pointed bill gave her head a triangular shape, while the broad shoulders and narrow tail used as a prop against the stump formed another triangle. Finally I knew what I meant by a giant triangular woodpecker.

❧❧❧

A year or two later, Sally and her husband Joe were paying us a winter visit. "What's that big bird on your ash tree down there?" Sally asked. "It looks like a woodpecker, but it's so big."

"It's a pileated woodpecker," I replied. He was so busy he seemed oblivious to anything but his work. Nevertheless, because we knew they are shy birds, we stayed quietly in the house. The bird was whacking off chunks of bark from the side of the tree facing us, so we had a perfect view.

His head moved rapidly from side to side. First a chip would fall from the left side, then the right, each one a little farther from the center. He was making the telltale rectangular excavation of his species. The pounding was so hard and fast that Sally wondered how his head could physically stand it. The answer lies in the peculiar bone structure of woodpeckers. The beak is very strong and the bone extends in one piece clear to the back of the head to absorb the shock.

Suddenly our pileated's head stopped going back and forth and concentrated on one spot near the middle, hammering away on that for several minutes. Because his movements were so quick, we couldn't tell whether he was getting any grubs or insect larvae to eat or not.

Abandoning that site, he hopped around to the other side of the tree, inspected several locations and finally flew into the woods upstream. Scientifically minded Joe went out and picked up some of the debris, chunks an inch long and a quarter inch through. He then stuck a twig into the tiny hole the woodpecker had made and measured its length. That bird had penetrated the trunk three inches.

"Why would a bird go to all that work unless he knew something was in there?" asked Joe.

"And how does he know where to hammer?" I wondered.

I called a University of Wisconsin ornithologist, one of my favorite KPs, who, of course, had the answers. "A woodpecker wouldn't dig that far into a wholly sound tree. There must have been some deterioration in the trunk at that point. In deciding where to excavate, woodpeckers use their sense of feel to a certain extent, as well as hearing and smell. We're just beginning to learn about birds' sense of smell. It's probable that they use it much more than heretofore believed."

Later I carefully looked over those two ash trees and found six other rectangular holes, obviously caused by other visits of this big bird. Right in front of the windows, not fifty feet away, and none of us had seen him. Nature's creatures are very secretive. Things can happen right under your nose that you never know about.

VIII.
Winter birds

"I'm concerned about my female cardinal," Margaret Perko, a fellow writer, told me one day. "She always waits until her mate is through eating before she comes in for her share of sunflower seeds."

"Just wait until spring," I said. "Not only will he let her feed at the same time, be will frequently give her an especially choice morsel."

"Well, okay," Margaret replied. "As a feminist I was worried about her, that's all."

I knew what she meant. Our male cardinal was also chauvinistic and he was often seen chasing off another male who dared to intrude. The female was equally inhospitable to her kind.

Eventually, during a period of deep snow and extreme cold, our dominant pair softened their stance. We began to see two or three males at a time, then three or four females. Usually they ate at a discreet distance from each other, but any skirmishes were brief and did not result in a bird being forced to leave the feeding area. Almost any winter day now when we wander past the windows we can see that cheery flash of red. Then at dusk four or more pairs often steal in together for a bedtime snack.

"I heard a cardinal singing this morning," Norm reported as he brought the morning paper in from the mailbox on a clear, bright

62   Clausen

January day. "It was singing the mating song, I think," he said, hanging his blaze-orange cap and jacket back in the closet.

"Did it sound like *what cheer, what cheer, what cheer! Birdie, birdie, birdie,*" I asked.

"Well, sort of."

Cardinals do not migrate but have been gradually extending their range northward. Seven states — Illinois, Indiana and others — have chosen this beauty for their state bird. Not only its color but its song is showy — a loud, cheerful warble.

Since the increase in the cardinal population at our feeder, it's been more common to see males and females feeding at the same time. Perhaps my friend Margaret can stop worrying — things are improving in the cardinal world.

❧❧❧

"This is better than watching TV!" is a comment we've heard more than once from a non-birder looking out the window at a succession of chickadees, juncos, goldfinches and woodpeckers at our seed and suet feeders.

In winter, juncos are our most faithful customers — those chubby little slate-gray fellows with the neat line on the breast between their outer and their under wear. The male is uniformly dark gray except for the contrasting white underparts. The female is lighter gray or brownish above. Outer tail feathers are white and show up prominently in flight.

"What's that bird?" my friend Sara asked one day as we sipped a cup of tea. "It looks like a junco, but it has some pink on the flanks."

As I checked into my faithful bird guide, I helped myself to some of the banana bread she had brought over. "That's a junco all right. They used to be called Oregon juncos but it's all one species now — the dark-eyed junco."

Juncos don't actually use the feeder itself. In flocks of ten or twenty, they hop about on the ground below and pick up seeds obligingly scattered by messier birds who feed upstairs. Because juncos have the finch-type bill, they can eat seeds with dispatch. After Norm scatters two or three handfuls of seeds on the ground in the morning, juncos are usually the first birds to come back to feed. Companionable, gregarious birds, snow and cold do not deter juncos; they have undoubtedly earned the right to be called snowbirds.

❧❧❧

"That looks like a sparrow under the feeder, but it's so small," Norm observed one winter morning. "I wonder what it is?"

It did not take long to find it on the sparrow pages of the bird guide — tree sparrow. He has a cinnamon cap and some soft gold color where his light breast meets the sparrow streaks on his back. A dark spot in the middle of his breast distinguishes him from our summer visitor, the chipping sparrow.

"He has a funny little hop while he feeds," Norm said. "He's not really scratching for seeds because they're right there in plain sight."

"He probably has to scratch like that in summer when his food is a little more elusive," I guessed.

Tree sparrows like the feeding table with its mix of small grains called wild bird seed. This is cheaper than the sunflower seed we put in the feeders and it is easier for some birds to eat.

Richard made that feeding table of his own unique design. The legs were made from trunks of a few of the surplus small oaks that keep invading our meadows. A fifth leg standing at center back is a young oak tree that extends six feet above the table, complete with all its branches. Birds often perch there before or after feeding.

❦❦❦

"Come quick, here's a tufted titmouse," I occasionally call out to anyone in earshot. But only occasionally. Their visits to our feeders are rare. Halfway between a junco and a chickadee in size, the titmouse seems more graceful than either with his long tail, slender body and perky crest. He is gray with white underparts and chestnut flanks. Perhaps his most appealing feature is his bright black eye, the more surprising because we are seldom aware of eye color in birds.

His visits to the feeder are usually brief. He snatches a seed and flies off into the underbrush to eat it in privacy. But one cold day when Kristin was visiting I called her to the front windows. "Do you want to see how a tufted titmouse eats? He doesn't have a finch-type bill but he doesn't have to work as hard as a blue jay to get a bite to eat."

We watched as with a whack or two he had the hull off and the seed in manageable pieces. I knew Kristin would be interested because we learned in ornithology class that the kind of bill a bird has determines what he can eat and how hard he has to work to get it.

❦❦❦

"We really ought to see an eagle today," Norm said on a bright, cold fall morning. Eagles usually arrive here from their northern nesting grounds sometime in November. Several people had told us they were seeing eagles — out near the bluffs, from Water Street or while crossing the Highway 12 bridge — but were we scanning the sky in vain.

Norm had made the same remark on several previous days, but

this day seemed different — the first really wintry one. When we sat down to breakfast in front of the windows, pink and purple clouds lit up the western horizon. They were a reflection of what was happening in the east as the sun rose over Blackhawk Ridge.

"Look at Ferry Bluff. It's as lit up as though a red spotlight was shining on it," I remarked between bites of toast. In another moment, it was in shadow, golden light playing on lower wooded riverbanks.

All the little birds checked into the feeding area early. Gulls and even crows were enjoying the strong winds, circling and soaring over the blue river. Crows don't really soar but they take advantage of the wind and sail a little now and then. The white bodies of gulls gleamed in the sun as they entertained us with an intricate ballet — the perfect setting for our elusive eagle.

"There he is!" Norm suddenly called out.

A magnificent adult eagle soared in from over the house, close enough that we could see his hooked beak and yellow feet clearly as he turned to catch the wind current. He followed the riverbank about five hundred yards upstream, pausing, turning, rising, falling. The sight of that dark body and white head and tail against a flawless blue sky never fails to quicken the pulse.

Was he going to land in one of our trees? No, he headed back downstream with a couple of powerful wing beats, passing once more above our heads before vanishing over the trees beyond. He must have known he was making a proclamation for an enraptured audience.

❊❊❊

Why do perfectly normal people who have seen eagles every winter for years get so excited over the first one each year? I like Pat Peckham's comment — something about hearing a brass band when he sees an eagle flying up the river.

One gloomy Sunday we were expecting our friends, the Kindschis and the Eberhardts, for a noon meal. We hoped the four bald eagles seated impassively in one tree on Eagle Point would stay around until they came.

The eagles didn't oblige but we humans lingered over dessert and coffee, enjoying pine siskins, goldfinches, chickadees and nuthatches with a cardinal and a red-bellied woodpecker for color. Sara Eberhardt watches avidly for eagles from her kitchen window in Sauk Prairie but neither she nor the others had seen any eagles this year.

The conversation turned to other matters when suddenly it was interrupted by Sara, who was pushing back her chair and pointing toward the river, almost speechless.

To Thank a River 65

"Oh... oh... there... there!" We all looked and finally she got it out: "My first eagle this year!"

❧❧❧

Every time the river floods, dead trees that have fallen from its banks are carried downstream. When the water level goes down, these trees or large branches make convenient perches for some birds. One dull gray winter morning, I noticed something different on one of those logs. I put down my spoonful of oatmeal and reached for the binoculars.

As I suspected, an immature eagle was perched there. Mottled brown, black and white, he wouldn't have that striking white head and tail until the age of four or five. Each year immature eagles gain more white, so it's possible to guess their age by coloring.

Another immature eagle came to join the first but immediately flew off. Since she was larger, I assumed she was a female. I lost track of her but later I saw the two of them seated companionably on another log. She must have decided he was good company after all.

Soon they both took off, flying about fifty feet apart, soaring and circling over the river. I watched their rhythmic flight for several minutes; wind currents must have been just right. They made ever-widening circles, flying on the perimeter opposite each other. When they were above tree-top level, they began to soar over the land, going higher and higher. Occasionally, on some secret signal, they would change places in the circle, flying past each other and continuing the spiral. Finally they were lost to sight over Blackhawk Ridge.

Jed had told us in ornitohology class that immature eagles practice mating flights in this fashion. Sometimes we see adults flying rhythmic patterns in the sky in January when the breeding season begins. A few fortunate people have seen them do their tumbling act. At the top of the flight, they clasp talons and begin to fall in slow cartwheels that gradually pick up speed, whirling and sliding to earth. At the last possible moment, they separate and swoop away. It's symbolic of their decision to be mates and with eagles they say it's for life.

To some of us, the mating flight of eagles is as spectacular as aerial acts in a circus and there's no admission charge. The only problem is figuring out how to be in the right place at the right time to witness it.

❧❧❧

Once during an unseasonable winter rain I noticed an eagle sitting on a log in shallow water near the opposite bank. As first, I thought he might be nearsighted and wanted to watch for his lunch at a more convenient level. He dipped his beak in the water — fishing? Taking a drink? He didn't appear to be eating anything.

Hopping off the log into the water, he settled down, spread his wings and splashed around. He looked rather ignominious, I thought, for a bird whose usual image is projected by sitting high in a tree looking haughty. The whole scene seemed strange and I began to wonder where to call to report a sick eagle.

As if to set my mind at ease, he lifted off and flew about twenty feet to some sand at the water's edge, where he began to preen himself. So maybe he was all right after all. But rain was still coming down. How was he going to get dry? Perhaps the mild weather prompted him to take a bath. But why in the rain? Maybe he prefers a shower bath.

❀❀❀

The wind chill we often experience here in winter is not popular with humans but it's made to order for eagles. One such day was brittle cold — blue sky, blue river carrying thin sheets of ice along, brilliant sunshine, trees bowing to an icy blast from the north.

Just upstream I noticed an immature eagle circling high in the sky. Then an adult. We had not seen many eagles that winter, so I called to Norm. "Come quick and see the eagles!"

We watched, fascinated, as two more immatures joined in. They made a magnificent sight against that sky. Not a wing moved as they circled and soared high over the river, making their way slowly downstream. When they were directly overhead, the uniformly mottled patterns of the immatures were particularly striking. The procession moved on. Just below our place, all five turned toward Blackhawk Ridge and disappeared.

"Why do you think we don't get tired of watching eagles?" I mused. We enjoy all the birds we see, but I think the only bird by which we are *awed* is the bald eagle. Perhaps it's the sheer size — seven and a half feet is a *lot* of wingspan. Perhaps it's because they visit us in winter, when we tend to get cabin fever. It's a tonic to let our imaginations soar with an eagle, free of our snowbound earth. The eagle is said to represent freedom, which probably has something to do with its having been chosen as our national symbol.

Back in 1904, a famous naturalist, John Burroughs, lamented the decline in numbers of this bird. He wrote: "Only a small proportion of Americans today have ever seen the emblem of their country flying above them, wild and free."

If you've ever seen an eagle in a zoo, you know it's not the same thing at all. I wonder if our new friends in Sauk Prairie really realize how privileged we all are?

To Thank a River

❧❧❧

One fall day I got an excited phone call from Dave Erickson. "I saw a golden eagle!" The field marks he described had convinced him it wasn't just an immature bald eagle. At that time, he and Judy lived a few miles down the river on the opposite bank and we used to keep each other informed of special sightings.

I had never seen a golden eagle very close up. I just thought of it as a big dark bird, not nearly as beautiful as a bald eagle. So I didn't really share Dave's enthusiasm, although I remembered all the birders were excited to have two on the Christmas bird count in 1984.

Golden eagles live in mountainous areas adjacent to open country where they can find good hunting for the small mammals they live on. During the nesting season, a pair will defend a large territory, as much as a whole township — thirty-six square miles. Afterward, they, especially the immatures, will wander more widely in search of food.

Our winter days seem to revolve around bald eagles — watching them soar from our windows, finding out where other people have been seeing them, spending time manning the telescope at the Lookout, going out at dusk to count eagles as they fly into the roost, or attending Eagle Council meetings. Toward spring the excitement dies down, sightings are rare and we miss those big, bold, beautiful birds.

One bright, windy March day, Juliana, Richard and I saw an eagle fly across the river and land briefly in a tree. "Was that an immature eagle?" Juliana wondered aloud.

But there was something different about it. It was so beautiful — golden brown wings and back with black wingtips. I dove for the bird guide while the others kept binoculars glued on the bird. "The tail is white with a black band on the end," Rich reported.

That clinched the identification — an immature golden eagle. He didn't stay long, but I can still visualize the golden-brown back and dark wingtips as the huge bird settled into that tree. This time it was my turn to call Dave. As I described what we had seen, he said, "You sound just like I did when I called you about one in the fall."

Now I know a golden eagle is not just a big dark bird. It's very special. Maybe he came to put a cap on the eagle season for us.

IX.
Water birds

During our first years here, we often skied up along the river to the big sandblow where the East Fork comes in. We used to enjoy that little trek, but we can't take it anymore because formerly open areas are completely overgrown — mostly with prickly ash, which makes them impassable. Nothing stands still in nature it seems.

At one of those early visits, on a sparkling January day, Kristin, Juliana, Norm and I were on that trail. As we skied up over a rise toward a shallow bay, we stopped abruptly at the sight of about twenty black and white ducks. As they took off like a squadron of fighter planes, their wings made a whistling sound. "What are those?" asked three voices at once.

"I think there are some ducks called whistlers," I replied. "Did you hear that sound when they flew?"

"It was a whistle, all right," Kristin said, zipping her down jacket against the wind coming off the river.

From our table at the window, where we often gather to eat, drink coffee or just to visit, we soon became acquainted with the black and white ducks that spend the winter here. We learned that if the duck in question had a white spot between the eye and the bill, it was a goldeneye, or "whistler."

Goldeneyes go up into Canada — the Hudson Bay area — or

even Arctic Alaska for the summer, so it's no wonder they can play around in our icy Wisconsin River so comfortably. They float backward, swing around and float frontward, take off and fly a few feet and then skid to a quick stop in the water. Just as I get binoculars set to study the markings on one, he disappears unceremoniously under water, never to reappear again, as far as I can tell.

A little research informed me that goldeneyes have a unique way of feeding. They can dive as deeply as ten feet, swimming with powerful strokes of their webbed feet. They eat many kinds of seeds, tubers and the stems and leaves of pondweed and wild celery. They also overturn stones to feed on crayfish, aquatic insects and shrimp-like crustacea.

If the duck in question didn't have that white spot between eye and bill, it usually turned out to be a male merganser, which is also predominantly black and white; but his head is more streamlined and he has a longer neck.

The goldeneye doesn't appear to have much of a neck at all. His puffy head is actually dark green at close range, his back is mostly black, neck and chest white. We seem to see more of the female goldeneyes, who are mostly gray with reddish heads. But some of these are no doubt first-year males, since they resemble females. When goldeneyes take flight, sunshine glistens on the white underparts and wings of both sexes. They usually fly very low over the water, straighter and faster than anything else we see passing by.

We relied on the prominent white cheek spot to distinguish quickly between goldeneye and merganser. One late winter day some friends were sitting at the table with us, watching the river go by and discussing where to go for our Friday night fish fry. "What's that duck?" asked Roger Winans as he nibbled some of my blue cheese dip and crackers.

No white dot, so, with my mind on calling somewhere for a dinner reservation, I casually answered "a merganser."

"Oh, no," said Dean Pawlisch, lapsing into hunting language. "Them's bluebills!"

Then I really looked. These ducks had dark chests, not white, like mergansers. With binoculars, I could see that the bill was broad, flat — and, yes — blue, not long and pointed. A quick peek in my trusty bird guide: "Greater scaup, migrating through," I admitted.

❊❊❊

"Those aren't mallards — that's something else," said Norm one spring morning, binoculars in hand. Two mallard-sized ducks were swimming slowly upstream, brown heads held high on long white necks. They made a striking picture; lighter brown bodies, white at

70   Clausen

the base of the tail, and a very unusual tail it was. Wedge-shaped, with two long dark central tail feathers curling upward at a jaunty angle.

It didn't take long to find this species in the bird guide. Quite appropriately, they are called pintails. More common in the western part of the country, they do migrate through here in spring and fall. Some occasionally winter in southern Wisconsin. Pintails breed from central Wisconsin north into the Arctic.

These pintail ducks feed mostly on vegetation, tipping up *(dabbling)* as mallards do. They also sometimes eat small aquatic animals. If frozen ponds greet the returning pintails, they will seek grain in farmers' fields.

The female is the usual nondescript mottled brown but she has a longer neck and a more pointed tail than, for example, the female mallard. These female ducks are nondescript, that is, unless one of them pauses long enough in morning sunlight for us to admire her subtle markings and soft brown and white coloring. Which is, of course, great camouflage when she is sitting on a nest.

❧❧❧

Spring brings shore birds. During our first year here, Kristin and I invited our ornithology class for one of our "woodcock parties." Everyone brought a dish to pass and after a satisfactory feast, we all went out into the East Meadow a little after sunset.

We walked slowly and silently to a place where I had heard woodcocks before and sat down in the sandy prairie to wait — carefully avoiding the prickly pear cactus. Jed brought his family along and I still remember how quietly the two and four year old children sat in their parents' laps. They had been bird-watching before.

Soon we heard what we had been waiting for: a harsh, nasal *peent* uttered at intervals. We couldn't quite see the woodcock but we knew he was strutting around an open spot near some brush where he hoped a female was hiding. Eventually we saw a small form shoot up in the air in ever widening circles and heard the melodic whistling of his wings. Higher and higher he went until he was completely out of sight.

"You'll hear a different sound when he comes down," Jed said softly.

What we heard was an ecstatic spring song. Our eyes strained to catch sight of the bird again as he came down in a precipitous, erratic plunge. Suddenly there he was, in almost the same spot, and the peenting began all over again.

We watched three more performances. "The woodcock will keep at this until a certain degree of darkness," Jed told us. "The candle power needs to be exactly right to inspire him. In the full moon, he often performs off and on all night."

Sometimes with binoculars we could just see the brownish, dumpy little bird with rounded wings, a short tail and an amazingly long, straight beak. "That beak is especially constructed for digging earthworms. The upper mandible can be moved away from the lower, even when it is plunged three inches into the soil," Jed explained.

These birds live near moist ground or bottomland and come north as soon as frost is out of the ground. If they come back too early, they can supplement their diet with insect larvae and occasional seeds and berries.

Like the killdeer, the woodcock is a marginal shore bird. He doesn't live in or on the water but nearby.

❃❃❃

I remember killdeers from my childhood, calling their name from the fields and pastures of southeastern Wisconsin. But I was to get reacquainted one day in late March when we were returning in our motorhome from our annual six weeks in the South. Four inches of heavy wet snow made our drive over the Military Ridge and through the hills and valleys of western Dane County look like fairyland. Norm, who claims he doesn't like cold weather anymore, remarked, "Florida doesn't have anything like this."

Along the highway we kept seeing small flocks of birds, but we had difficulty identifying them because, as we approached, they inevitably scattered. Eventually, we decided that many were robins and others were blackbirds. With normal food sources under a blanket of snow, they were scrounging what they could on the relatively clear road.

Other flocks puzzled us. I thought of horned larks, who do a lot of such feeding along roads in winter. But these were a little too large. Something about the way they flew reminded us of shore birds we had seen along the ocean. The black and white wing pattern was similar to that in willets and sanderlings.

Then I saw something I had missed before — a diamond-shaped, rust-colored rump patch, outlined at the base of the tail in black and white. I dove for the bird book and looked in the shore bird family. It was not hard to find — the good old midwestern killdeer. In all my years of seeing and hearing killdeer, never before had I spotted that striking rump patch.

Next we confirmed two black collars around their white necks. "But some have only one stripe," Norm said. His role is to keep watching while I search the bird guide.

"The semipalmated plover has only one stripe. He migrates

72 Clausen

through here — and so does the piping plover. But the piping is a rare sighting — an endangered species," I reported. "That would be exciting."

But then I read further: "Adult killdeer has two neck bands, juvenile only one." So that settled that. Just a flock of adult and juvenile killdeer who came back north a day or so too soon. Which proves once again that you can always learn something new about an old friend.

❦❦❦

A large dark bird rose slowly from the water on the other side of the river about 7:15 one spring morning. "That's an osprey; he has wings with that bent-elbow look," I said. "But what's he trying to carry?"

"It's a fish — a really big one," Norm replied.

The bird flew around a bit, apparently seeking a good landing place for himself and his prize. Eventually he settled in one of the taller trees across the river. After adjusting the telescope in that direction, we could plainly see the fish tightly clamped under his talons. The fish hung down from the branch, his tail flapping a moment before becoming quiet. "That fish must weigh three pounds," Norm said.

The osprey bent over at frequent intervals and took a few bites. For the next hour we checked the telescope occasionally, and he was having a good meal. By 8:30, he was gone but there was a lot of fish left.

The underparts of an osprey are mostly white, with dark patches at the crook of the wings. There is some white on the head, which might cause confusion with an eagle. But an eagle's wingspan is as much as two feet wider; and his wings, which are broader, are held out absolutely flat when he flies.

We usually see osprey in April and May and then again in August through September. "Our" osprey probably breed in northern Wisconsin but this species is found almost worldwide; they breed in the western mountains, on the West Coast and up into Canada and Alaska. They winter in Florida, along the Gulf Coast, and down into South America.

Osprey build large stick nests in trees or nesting platforms and add to them year after year. Usually three eggs are laid and one brood is raised, both parents sharing in their care. The male feeds the female from the beginning of the pair bond until all the eggs are laid. Research has shown a relationship between well-fed female birds and their reproductive output.

Unlike eagles, osprey limit their diet to fish. Our old canoeing partners, Tom and Diana Webb, were acquainted with osprey but had never observed them actually fishing. One September day we canoed down the river together. As we sat on a high bank eating our lunch, Diana said, "Look at that osprey hovering."

Suddenly he plunged precipitously, folding his wings just as he entered the water. He immersed completely but came up without a fish. This bird, however, was not easily discouraged. He entertained us all through our lunch with several more spectacular dives. Finally he came up with a fish and flew off to enjoy his own lunch, just as we were finishing ours.

"That was quite a show you Clausens arranged for us," Tom remarked as we packed up to resume the trip.

❧❧❧

One summer morning at breakfast I caught sight of some movement on the sand across the river, but couldn't tell exactly what was over there. All I could see were the usual driftwood and grasses. At first I couldn't see anything more, even with binoculars, but suddenly a piece of driftwood moved a little.

There was a great blue heron, motionless in the shallow water. He stands four feet tall, so straight, thin and blue-gray that you think he's part of the scenery. Eventually I picked out three heron, each one occasionally moving upstream. Soon they were hidden behind the trees that, in summer, block our upstream view.

After breakfast, I walked to a better vantage point. With the naked eye, I could again see only inanimate objects. With binoculars, however, I eventually picked out four of the rangy gray creatures, seemingly just standing on the shore to enjoy the morning sun.

A long drawn-out harsh honking sound drew my eyes skyward. Three more heron flew in and settled down to join those on the beach. As they stood there, some heads were pulled in, some were elevated and alert. Occasionally one would lift his wings, rise a couple of feet off the ground and settle down again a short distance away. It must have been this sort of movement that attracted my attention in the first place.

I checked on the birds several more times that morning. Each time I would think there was nothing there until I searched with binoculars. One bird stood facing the other way, with his head pulled in, resembling an old-fashioned preacher, gray cloak pulled about him, head bowed in prayer.

Sometimes it took a while to find all seven birds. They spread out, some feeding in the shallows and some on land. They eat snakes, insects, mice and frogs as well as small fish. I wonder how many times that driftwood across the river has actually been a great blue heron that we didn't see?

When heron arrive early in April, they work on nest-building, often adding to one used in previous years. The male brings large sticks which the female puts in place. The finished product is two to three feet in diameter. I think there must be a small colony of heron nesting on the East Fork. They like privacy and unless the river is high enough for canoes to get through, wild creatures have this place all to themselves.

The only other large gray bird with which a great blue heron might be confused is the sandhill crane. The crane, however, has a red spot on his head, while the heron has a drooping black crest in back, which is usually visible. In flight, the crane's head is outstretched while the heron has his tucked in an S-shape.

In years of shallow water, blue heron sometimes inhabit our side of the river. One gray November morning with gentle rain falling, I noticed a stick or part of a bush down at the water's edge that reminded me of a great blue heron. It was a long stick leaning out over the water, and yes, it did come from the perfectly elliptical body of a great blue heron.

"That can't be a blue heron. I though they'd flown south weeks ago," I said to Norm. However, two pairs of binoculars trained on the bird proved that it was, indeed, a great blue.

To the record books: Yes, a very few blue heron stay in southern Wisconsin during winter; they have been seen on the Christmas bird count in Madison. "There's no reason why they couldn't stay, if they had a safe place to wait out winter storms near open water," Norm said.

A great blue heron can look comical, majestic or grotesque, depending on what he does with that long thin neck. It's just as long as his body. Ours stayed several minutes, striking his majestic pose, intently eyeing the water.

When he scrunched his head down for a few moments so his neck disappeared, he looked like a completely different bird. Head out again, immobilized — and then a quick jab into the water with that long spike of a beak. He must have caught a small fish; he swallowed it easily. One more morsel was eaten before he slowly turned and began a patient march along the shallow water and out of our sight. All his movements are graceful and deliberate, except for that lightning jab. We appreciated catching a glimpse of him, because as it turned out he did not choose to spend the winter with us.

❧❧❧

October brings the wild honking that tells us Canada geese are overhead again. Somehow it's not as exciting as when it is the long-awaited first sign of spring. But it seems to fit well with the first tinges of orange and yellow in maples and birch, and the first mornings with silver frost on the grass.

On one of those October days, I called to Norm: "There are ten Canada geese on the sandbar across the river."

They strutted self-importantly about, and during late afternoon they fed on the small amount of vegetation growing there. "It looks as though they are pecking away at sand," Norm said. "They probably need that for their crops."

The Canada goose is a heavy bird, weighing five to eight pounds, with a wingspread of about five feet. Brownish gray back, light-colored breast, long black neck and head with a long white patch on the side of the head — it's an easy bird to identify. They fly with a slow, powerful wing beat, unlike ducks, which are much smaller and whose wings beat much faster.

Most of these geese are on their way to their winter homes in southern Illinois or down along the Gulf Coast. There are three refuges in Illinois, maintained with revenue from hunting licenses. Here special feed is planted to carry the geese through the winter — clover, corn, wheat, millet and sorghum. Pampered, that's what they are!

Breeding grounds for geese are Canada and Alaska, as far north as the Arctic coast. Most of "our" geese are said to nest in the Hudson Bay area. Authorities tell us that in migration they fly as much as a mile a minute at altitudes up to nine thousand feet.

"I wish those geese would spend the night," I said as the sun set over downstream trees.

They wandered around and discussed it for a while. Two or three geese even settled down in the sand, as if to cast their vote for remaining. Others faced resolutely upstream. "They are voting for the fields of corn around the Horicon Marsh," Norm said.

Occasionally one goose would flap and stretch his wings. Then they all gathered in a cluster, as though for a caucus. The next time we looked they were standing in line, all facing upstream. When finally it grew almost too dark to see them, they spread their wings and flew honking into the night.

X.
Flowers

Flowers are more accommodating than birds. They sit still while you key them out and photograph them. But even they don't always show up in the same place year after year.

"I'm going out to look for a sign of spring," I told Norm one blustery, gray April day.

"Today?" he said, hardly glancing up from the sports page. "Good luck!"

Our dry, sandy prairie doesn't produce the charming spring ephemerals I used to enjoy as a child. Spring comes more subtly here. I knew just where the first sign should be, a few feet off to the right of the Spirit Trail near two young oak trees.

And there, just peeking through sand and dead oak leaves, I found it — about eight hairy green buds nestled together, close to the earth. Pasqueflowers! They are also known as Easter flower, wild crocus, or sometimes windflower.

I knew they should be there, because I had planted the seeds in 1975. The oaks were small then, but they served to mark the spot. It was sunny, dry, well-drained, sandy — just what pasqueflowers need to thrive. But the pasqueflowers did not come up the next year, nor the one after that. Aprils came and went — ten of them — with no sign of the pasqueflowers.

Finally in 1986 the first miracle occurred. Two tiny buds appeared, followed by blossoms two inches across with about six white-to-lavender petals. The next year there were three blossoms and, since then, a thriving plant, with more blossoms each year.

On that particular April day the buds were crowded together on the ground like newborn baby birds trying to keep warm.

The story goes that they look so furry that they were called goslings by prairie children. The full-blown petals are hairy on the under side. In May or June, the orange center produces seeds, each one borne on a hairy filament about an inch and a half long. By that time, the plant has also produced large, finely divided, feathery looking leaves. On that blustery day, the goslings were proof for me that the miracle would happen once again and spring would eventually appear.

When it did, the next floral sign of spring was the early buttercup. The tiny, waxy yellow faces peeked at us from all sorts of odd places — in the lawn, at the edge of the meadow path — anywhere that they weren't hampered by taller, older vegetation.

Early in our tenure of our river property, a trip to the Schluckebier Prairie on the other side of the river introduced me to prairie smoke. This plant produces clouds of delicate pinkish-lavender "smoke" hovering six or eight inches off the ground. Each plant has many graceful gossamer plumes, seemingly without much more substance than real smoke.

"We have to have a whole field of prairie smoke!" I announced to the family, who accepted my decision with somewhat less enthusiasm than I had for the project. But how would I get prairie smoke? Collecting seed and planting it sounded like a long, laborious process. Then I heard about an old prairie whose owner had decided to plow it up to plant something prosaic like corn. We were welcome to take anything we could transplant — and there was plenty of prairie smoke.

I persuaded Kristin to help me dig some plants, and Norm to help me plant them. Two weeks later I was proudly showing off the newly transplanted prairie smoke with its tiny raspberry-colored buds. Two weeks after that I couldn't find it; that growth had all died out. However, new green shoots eventually came up; all was not lost.

The second spring, raspberry-colored buds appeared on our five clumps in April, followed in May by those gossamer plumes I so admired. Ever since, the prairie smoke has spread and bloomed luxuriantly. One year Kristin came in from a tour of the prairie and reported excitedly: "Mom! I counted forty-three clumps of prairie smoke in bloom! They are on both sides of the path through the East Meadow."

Eventually I learned that those raspberry-colored buds were ac-

78   Clausen

tually the flowers. White petals are hidden inside the deep pink bracts and sepals, but are seldom seen because the flower opens only enough for pollination. Seeds are borne at the end of these long plumes, which are finely hairy and account for the name prairie smoke.

❧❧❧

"It's getting warm out there. I didn't need this," Norm said one late May morning as he hung up that old plaid jacket with holes in the sleeves. "I can see why you say puccoon looks like vases of flowers all over the prairie."

Putting away the last of the breakfast dishes, I said "I think the name *puccoon* just suits those flowers, don't you?"

The bright yellow blossoms are not delicate in appearance or color. The plant is sturdy, with plenty of plain, narrow, lance-like leaves in a reliable shade of green marching up the substantial stems. They are a foot high or so, and tend to grow in groups of ten or twelve, with the blossoms at the very top — hence the "vases of flowers" appearance.

Puccoon does stand out when the meadow is in its early summer green. Nature, like an interior decorator, picks up the same hue in some of her carpeting. Tiny dwarf cinquefoil, which grows everywhere except in deep grass, is a paler reflection of the same color.

Four or five flower heads containing several blossoms or buds appear at the top of each puccoon stem. The flowers are tubular, breaking into an uncomplicated face of five petals, protected at the base by five small green calyxes. Puccoon is in the forget-me-not family, and one can see that the petals are similar. It is called hoary puccoon because the stems are covered with fine hairs, giving them a frosty or hoary look.

An almost brassy yellow, it announces its presence like silent trumpet calls from all over the East Meadow.

In a few more days we find another yellow flower on the upper river path, the first goatsbeard pointing its cheerful face to the sun. Later it will have an airy seedhead like an ordinary dandelion but larger. Marian, my friend and early mentor, used to collect the seedheads for dried bouquets, using hair spray to preserve them. The flower has a spiky appearance because a long green bract sticks out beneath each of the dozen or so yellow petals. In the center are many tiny black stamens topped with yellow.

Closer to the ground we find many dwarf dandelions, six or eight inches tall. They are a native plant, a different family from the common dandelion. The flat yellow blossom is at the top of a slender stem growing from tiny basal leaves which vaguely resemble those of

To Thank a River

the common dandelion. Growing everywhere is rock cress, six to twelve inches high, with four dainty white petals.

My neighborhood walking group often shifted our attention from birds to flowers, especially when birding was slow. "What's this tiny blue flower?" asked Mary one day. "It has a lipped blossom like a penstemon or lobelia."

We puzzled over it. There was no penstemon that small. It most resembled a brook lobelia. "But what would a brook anything be doing in this dry sandy soil?" I wondered.

Diane had a different flower guide. After flipping a few pages she suggested, "Maybe it's blue toadflax."

Sure enough, there it was, tiny narrow leaves and all. Our guidebook says: "Suggests a small lobelia but note the slender spurs." I must say I couldn't really see any spurs; the blossom is minuscule.

Dwarf dandelion, rock cress and blue toadflax are tiny plants that grow only a few inches tall. In one spot near the edge of the woods we sometimes find a small garden of all three varieties. It is a symphony of color. Well, maybe not a symphony, but at least a string quartet.

***

"What grows to be six feet tall, has both male and female plants, with the showiest flowers on the male?" I tossed out the question just as Norm was leaving for the golf course, but his mind was not really on flowers.

He was more interested later in the day as we took an early summer walk along the lower river path. I challenged him: "Did you know there's a drug called thalicarpine, used in cancer research, that is made from seeds of that tall plant?"

Called meadow rue, it likes moist places and stream banks. An eye catcher, it towers above surrounding vegetation and is sometimes called "maid of the mist." The fluffy white male flowers do not have petals. They are a mass of tiny, delicate white stamens hanging from individual slender stems. Female plants have inconspicuous purple sepals and a few elongated purplish pistils. The leaves resemble columbine, with leaflets less than one inch wide, usually with three lobes at the end.

I once read about a couple who moved to some acreage in northern Wisconsin to escape the hassles of city life. Finding a lot of meadow rue on the property, they named the place *Meadow Ruh,* spelling it like the German word for peace. *Ruhig* (peaceful) certainly describes our riverbank on a quiet June morning.

"What a funny name! Why would a flower be called a spiderwort?" visitors sometimes ask.

"Don't let that turn you off," I tell them. "Notice how long and graceful the foliage is — sort of spidery. And the Anglo-Saxon word for plant is *wort.*"

The purple-blue blossoms and graceful foliage of spiderwort gladden our roadsides and fields for several weeks each spring and early summer.

Few plants on the acreage are so generous with their bloom. Each slender stalk has one or two flower heads, containing from six to twenty-eight green buds. Anywhere from one to four flowers on one stem will open on a given morning, an exquisite *fleur-de-lis.* Each center holds six tiny yellow stamens surrounded by deep purple fringe.

I do enjoy my spiderwort, but it's a will-o'-the-wisp. It has a will of its own, an independent spirit. I can feast my eyes on an acre of the misty blue lovelies. But if I phone Sara and say, "Come and see the meadow today. It's out of this world," there may or may not be a show when she comes. We may be greeted by slender stalks, spidery foliage and tight fists of tiny green buds.

I think I've figured out their timetable. Sometimes they are out on cloudy days, sometimes sunny ones. But on a really hot day, about noon they begin to turn dark purple and withdraw from this world. Evidently they respond to temperature changes.

❈❈❈

"How does a tightly closed flower like that ever get pollinated?" asked a neighbor one day. We were admiring one of our showiest prairie plants. It is called wild indigo, and I'm very proud of it, because one of my prairie mentors, Donald Kindschi, tells me it's a sign of true prairie. I didn't plant it, either; it came by itself.

My wild indigo is about four feet tall. The sturdy, smooth green stems with a bluish bloom each support several flower-carrying spikes which spring from purplish nodes. The purple color carries along the inside of the stems to give the whole plant a grayish-lavender look.

In August, the large, pea-like pods turn black, and the leaves turn black to match. Seeds are very tiny, but they make an audible rattle in winter winds. Native Americans used them as rattles for babies to play with. It is sometimes called rattle pod.

"Now you can see how that flower gets pollinated," I said as a bee buzzed in and began methodically visiting the white, pea-like blossoms.

The bee grabbed an upper petal with two front legs and pulled the two lower petals down with his other legs, gradually forcing his head deep inside. Even the largest blossoms appeared tightly closed

To Thank a River

until he arrived, and snapped shut with conviction as soon as he left. "Bee gets nectar, and the next plant gets pollinated," commented my neighbor. "Pretty clever."

❦❦❦

My friend Joe Benforado — of the scientific mind — left me a note one day when he and Sally had been staying here during our absence. "I don't think that's a penstemon in the East Meadow. Look up germander in your flower guide." I walked out toward the pines to look for this plant with its showy lavender spikes. He's right; the distinguishing characteristic of germander is that the stamens protrude through a cleft in the upper lip of the blossom. Actually the stamens look like antennae on an insect.

But I find another flower with showy lavender spikes that looks like a penstemon, lobelia, snapdragon type. The leaves are narrow, toothed, opposite; flowers are tubular with a dotted lower lip. It's not a penstemon, because that species has two upper lobes that turn up; this flower has a single lobe that turns down. Turtlehead catches my eye, but that is white. I look up *red turtlehead,* but that's not it either.

Next to it is a picture of dragonhead, and that description fits perfectly. It is in the mint family; sure enough, the stem is square. If I had checked the stem earlier, my search would have been shorter! My guide says dragonhead is sometimes known as obedient plant, because when you push a blossom to one side, it stays that way. I try it often and it always fascinates visitors, especially children.

Identifying each plant and bird as they show up in their own season is like being a detective. It's not necessary to wear a trench coat, but sometimes the magnifying glass comes in handy.

My friends the Appleyards started their prairie about the same time I did mine, but theirs is much more colorful. They have lots of bergamot. Its lavender blossoms would be just what I need to brighten up my prairie, which some years is mostly green and white. Bergamot has many tiny lavender tubular flowers almost an inch long. The tube splits open about half way out, and half the ends are shaggy, giving the whole a rather helter skelter appearance. Long, oval-pointed leaves in pairs climb the square sten. Yes, it's a mint.

The scientific name is *Monarda fistulosa.* Monardes was a Spanish physician who wrote widely in the sixteenth century about medicinal uses of New World plants. Fistulosa means "like a reed or pipe," and refers to the tubular shape of the flowers.

Jane Appleyard has offered to let me collect some bergamot seed, but somehow when the time is right we both forget it. I may have neglected to plant bergamot, but one summer day while walking along

82 Clausen

the lower river path I saw a splash of lavender color halfway up the bank: about ten beautiful bergamot blossoms. I know not whence came the seed, but I heartily thank whatever wind or bird planted it. However, I haven't seen it since. Another will-o'-the-wisp!

❧❧❧

Just what is a weed? Gardeners and farmers know, but botanists are not so sure. Perhaps it takes a philosopher to make such decisions. One of my favorite flower guides is called *Wildflowers and Weeds,* by Courtney and Zimmerman, but they don't tell you which are flowers and which are weeds.

When Kay Lindblade was here on a mid-summer weekend, she asked "What are those white flowers growing all over the East Meadow? I'd love to take some home for my dinner party tomorrow!"

"That's flowering spurge," I told her. "Of course you may pick some, but wild flowers don't always hold up well in the house."

Flowering spurge sprinkles its white umbels through the green grasses like stars in the milky way. Each individual floweret has five dainty white petals, shading to green at the center. If you take a magnifying glass, you can see the cluster of infinitesimal yellow stamens in the middle.

An even more insignificant-looking plant which grows here in profusion is called whorled milkweed, and you'll really need a magnifying glass to appreciate the intricate detail. It's called whorled because the leaves come out in whorls, or circles, all the way up the stem. The leaves are needle-like, and early in spring one visitor thought they were tiny pine trees.

The flowers are what make it easily identified as a milkweed. They are a greenish-white miniature of the lavender blossoms of the common milkweed. Five petals drop gracefully downward like a ballet skirt, while five even tinier, rounder petals form cups for the pistil and stamens. Even if man could make such a flower as perfect in every detail, it wouldn't reproduce itself. Yet every summer thousands of them appear like magic for us to enjoy. Now is that a flower or a weed?

❧❧❧

Shifting sands caused by flood waters bring surprises to the riverbank. We never know what flower will visit each summer. I say visit because spring floods carry the seeds or plants downstream to someone else's riverbank each year, and bring us new ones.

Years ago when I read August Derleth's description of a cardinal flower, I longed to find one for myself, especially since he said they were becoming scarce. I was less than pleased, however, when I saw my first one. A visitor brought it back from a canoe trip along the banks of the river one August. He had actually plucked that sacred flower! He seemed so pleased with his prize that I held back my consternation.

Since then we have occasionally had the pleasure of finding one or two cardinal flowers on our own stretch of river bank, but they don't show up often. One year while Norm and I were canoeing upstream we came upon a secret cove, surrounded by thick undergrowth.

"Look at that! Blue asters, white asters, dragonhead. It looks like a carefully planned garden!" I exclaimed.

We let the canoe drift and feasted our eyes on these attention-getters. "And there's a cardinal flower!" Norm pointed out.

Eventually we realized there were several tall stems crowned with slender, graceful cardinal flowers. That red, a deep scarlet, is so intense that it's a good thing the petals are slender, and there are only five of them. Two stretch sidewise, as though poised for flight, and the other three spread gently downward. The plants stand proudly, three or four feet tall, as though waiting for you to catch sight of them and marvel. Once you've spotted them, your eyes are drawn back again and again.

We visited a week later, and found even more cardinal flowers. The next August we came again.

"Where was that flower garden cove?" we asked each other. But the river had changed everything. The secret cove and the cardinal flowers were not there. Another will-o'-the-wisp!

❀❀❀

"Oh, look at all that goldenrod! Poor Douglas; he has hay fever," Jan Olson remarked when she got out of the car with her two-year-old son on a hot August day.

"No, goldenrod is innocent," I assured her. "But I'm afraid there is a lot of ragweed; that's what causes the allergy problems." I went on to explain, "Goldenrod has to be pollinated by insects and doesn't disseminate any pollen into the air. But it has been blamed for years because it blooms about the same time as ragweed and is much more visible."

We are apt to greet that first airy goldenrod with "Oh, it's too early for fall!" I checked my local flower guide and found that of the twelve varieties that bloom here, seven begin to bloom in July and the rest in August.

Twelve species? I thought it was all just goldenrod. A challenge!

Pictures and descriptions can be confusing, but sometimes reading the fine print in the flower guides is helpful. The Peterson guide divides the blossoms into shapes — plume-like, elm-branched, clublike and showy, wand-like and slender, and flat-topped. That helps. Another thing to check: are the leaves feather-veined (many veins coming off a midrib) or parallel-veined (few veins parallel to midrib)?

Turns out that most of my goldenrod is parallel-veined. Of the four parallel-veined species listed, only one is included in my local guide — Canada goldenrod. One of the guides calls it plume-like, the other arching. Either one could apply to this species, and with parallel-veining for the clincher, I am convinced it is Canada goldenrod, a native species. Somehow I appreciate the sunny look it gives the prairie even more now that I've sifted through twelve species to identify it.

❀❀❀

"What do you call that yellow sunflower type flower?" asked Juliana as we walked along the sandy river shore one quiet sunny August morning.

"Sneezeweed," I replied. "That's one I can remember because of the square-tipped petals. See how each petal has three notches? And the petals droop a little." So far as I know, this plant has nothing to do with making anyone sneeze. Perhaps it got its reputation like goldenrod, by being highly visible at the time that ragweed pollen is filling the air and making people miserable.

"And what's that one?" Juliana persisted. It had leafy stems two feet tall or so, with several four-petal bright yellow blossoms at least an inch across.

"That's evening primrose," I told her. "You can always identify it by the stigma projections in the form of a cross at the end of the pistil." Stamens and pistil are also yellow. This flower is found up in the meadows, as are the next two that caught our eyes: the ubiquitous daisy fleabane and some wandering sprays of butter'n'eggs.

❀❀❀

Kristin, my botanizer, surprised me one day. "Mom, did you know that two species of smartweed grow down here at the edge of the river?"

"I know smartweed all right. It has spikes of tightly packed pink blossoms. But I never found two kinds."

"One is called lady's thumb according to this flower guide," Kristin said, and showed me. "It says it has 'knotted stems with a papery shield at each joint.' I think I can see what they mean. The other species is called pale or dock-leaf smartweed, and it has no papery shield. And look at this," she pointed out. "The lady's thumb blossoms are erect, but the others tend to flop over. It all checks out with the guide book."

I could see that, even if I couldn't tell what they meant by a papery shield. No, I certainly hadn't noticed such minuscule differences in those pretty pink flowers that appear in the sandy shore late every summer.

I'm sure canoers drifting by are appreciating the blue river and sky, warm sun and cool breeze. Too bad they can't see all the colorful little treasures hidden along the green shores.

❧❧❧

In spite of some warm, sunny days, September nights are frosty. Not freezing; just frosty. Along with the season comes the frost aster. A clump which looks like a bouquet of snowflakes grows not far from the porch.

Wild asters have tiny flowers, but they have a lot of personality. On a walk in the West Meadow I found some heath asters. These tiny white flowers are so numerous at the end of the stem that they form a pyramid. The leaves are also crowded on the stem and look a bit like heather, tiny and stiff.

Grasses are all turning to tawny fall colors, which makes these white asters stand out crisp and fresh, reminiscent of spring. Close to the river is a mowed path leading downstream to the neighbor's house. One year it was bordered along almost half its length by a hedge of frost asters about three feet tall. Another will-o'-the-wisp, washed out by spring floods. The next year our frost asters were scattered here and there.

The individual flowers of frost aster are only about three quarters of an inch across, but their numerous perky white petals centered by deep yellow stamens are perfection in minuscule design. No two are alike. Some are just opening up, and the ones that are wide open appear to have separate personalities. Individual petals have their own ideas how and where they wish to stand in their little world, giving a whimsical look to the row of flowerets marching up the stem. This description could probably fit several of the white asters. To differentiate frost aster, I look for a hairy stem and arching branches.

Several varieties of beautiful blue asters grow in dry prairies, but not in ours. After searching in vain for a blue one for several years, I finally found one scrubby little specimen, near our property line. There, on the other side of the invisible boundary, were several clumps of brightly blooming blue asters. Now why would they show favoritism like that?

86 Clausen

※※※

One sunny June day we found an exquisite little flower almost hidden in the grasses of the East Meadow. On a slender stem six or eight inches high grew a five-petaled yellow flower about an inch across. A little research convinced me it was frostweed, a member of the rockrose family.

That year in November, Wayne Pauly, a Dane County naturalist, was walking our acres with us when he found a plant bearing many tiny seed heads on a wiry stem. "Frostweed," he told us. "That's one of the flowers I talk about in my folklore class."

It certainly didn't look like the plant with a single flower I had admired early in the summer. My flower guide later enlightened me: "Later, clusters of flowers without petals appear on branches." Those flowers were now tiny seedheads. There certainly are a variety of ways for plants to reproduce themselves.

As we meandered on, Wayne suddenly exclaimed, "Look at this. I've been searching for it for eight years! That's why they call it frostweed." He was down on his knees looking at one of the wiry stems.

Around its base was a graceful cone that looked like ice, although there was no other visible ice or snow. The temperature, however, was well below freezing and had been for at least twenty-four hours. Looking around we saw several more ice cones on frostweed.

"What is it? Where did it come from?" Norm and I immediately asked.

"It's just what it looks like, ice," he replied. We all tasted some to convince ourselves.

"That's what folklore said this plant would do. But I have no idea where the ice comes from. Folklore doesn't explain things very often." As we examined the fanciful shapes of several ice cones, for a few moments we were all back in an earlier time. We half expected an elf to peek around a tree and explain the phenomenon to us.

※※※

I've always thought of November as a bittersweet month. The north wind can be bitter, and on another day the November sun on your back can be sweet. It is the time of year when we treasure what color is left in the landscape, especially that delicious shade known popularly as bittersweet.

Not only is there the berry itself, but I "collect" the color whenever I come across it. As I entered the house with an armload of wood the other night, this favorite color greeted me flamboyantly in the flames in the wood stove. When I am busy in the kitchen, Norm

To Thank a River 87

often calls my attention to the tracery of bare branches against the sunset sky above Ferry Bluff. It is often vibrant with that same bittersweet color, reflected like shimmering silk in the river. Once in a while even in November I come across a particularly hardy maple which has retained some of its brilliant leaves.

Coming upon a patch of bittersweet on a hike in the country is always a lift for the spirits. Ordinarily we see it fairly close to the ground, but it is actually a twining woody vine and can climb as high as thirty feet. We once found a good crop growing at least twenty feet high in a tree in Blackhawk Ridge, very safe from predators. Bittersweet is protected in Wisconsin, and should not be picked unless it is on your own property. Not only does it provide us with a cheering flash of color on a dull November afternoon, but it furnishes food for birds during winter.

"Why don't we notice bittersweet until November?" Norm mused one day.

I looked in my flower guide and found some answers. "The flowers in June are an inconspicuous yellow-green," it said. "By September the yellow capsule is growing round and fat, giving no hint of the bright orange-scarlet seed inside."

One year I tried bringing some into the house a little early to watch the three parts of the capsule split open and reveal its secret. But those berries shriveled up. The ones that remained on the vine became perfect specimens.

Bittersweet is listed as emergency food in *Edible Wild Plants of North America* by Fernald and Kinsey. Chippewa Indians boiled the tender branches to get rid of the poisonous saponin in the bark, the resulting food being "sweet and palatable." I don't think I'll try fixing that for supper.

I'd rather just look at it, and let the birds eat it. At any rate, the fire in the wood stove and the bittersweet in my winter bouquet help make November more sweet than bitter for me.

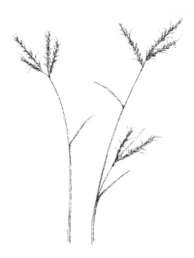

XI.
Trees

"For a great tree death comes as a gradual transformation." Edwin Way Teale, a well-known naturalist, said it. One of my favorite trees has been dead for many years. It was taller than surrounding trees, making it easy to identify birds perched on the bare branches. Glancing up at that silhouette against a sunset sky made preparing the evening meal or washing dishes a pleasant chore.

I agree with Teale: "Even when life has abandoned it entirely it remains a majestic thing... Alone among living things it retains its character and dignity after death. Plants wither; animals disintegrate. But a dead tree may be as arresting, as filled with personality, in death as it is in life."

But I can no longer raise my eyes to gaze at that familiar pattern of branches. A couple of weeks ago we noticed that the giant had fallen. When I went out to inspect the remains, I was surprised to find that the trunk had split in half, each half falling in the opposite direction. It must have just disintegrated.

There was neither leaf nor bark to verify that it was an oak, but the biggest and oldest trees on the place are all oaks. I paced off the spread of its crown and the length of the trunk. According to my rough estimate, the crown was forty feet across and the tree was about 45 feet tall. Tiny fungi march along the fallen trunk, and I'm sure many insects are busy helping to transform its wood into rich soil.

As Teale put it, in a tree's final moments, "It arrives at a fitting and noble end."

Trees sometimes give us the first inkling a long winter is finally ending. "I'm ready for spring," Juliana said one day. "Let's go look for pussy willows."

"We might find some," I replied. "On my way into Madison the other day I noticed weeping willow branches are turning chartreuse."

Actually the first sign of spring is something I never noticed until my friend Kate Lettau called it to my attention. She was secretary of the Wisconsin Phenological Society for many years. Now that's a rather forbidding name, but she made it interesting. Phenologists explain that spring progresses in an orderly fashion every year, and the flowering silver maple starts the season off in southern Wisconsin. She told me to look up, not down, for the first sign of spring — those lacy red flowers at the ends of twigs on the silver maple tree.

I found them, but remarked to Kristin later, "I didn't know trees had flowers."

"All trees have some kind of flower," she said. "Not very conspicuous, maybe, but that's how they reproduce themselves." Perfectly logical, but somehow the fact had previously escaped me.

❧❧❧

"What kind of a tree do you think that is?" I asked my two preschool grandsons as we took a winter walk many years ago. "A pine," promptly replied five-year-old Peter. "'S a pine," echoed Aaron, who was almost three.

I pulled off a twig. "See how the needles grow in clusters," I explained. "How many are there?" Peter carefully counted five needles.

"That's how you can tell it's a white pine," I announced importantly. Peter solemnly nodded. Aaron was unimpressed. "See, they're sort of soft and flexible," I continued from my store of information. "And if you look up at the tree it seems to have shelves. The branches come out straight and even, like shelves."

Later we saw how a red pine had longer, stiffer needles in clusters of two, and how the branches curved more and were more irregular so they didn't look so much like shelves. "I want to take home one of those twigs," said Peter.

Next stop was a river birch, with its curly, peeling bark. "See who can be the first to run to another one just like it," I suggested. That was easy for Peter; he was there before Aaron had figured out what I meant.

Last we came to an oak tree with its deeply fissured gray bark with many dried leaves clinging to its branches. I didn't bother to explain that pointed lobes on the leaves meant it was either a black or

90 Clausen

a red oak. The boys were too busy looking to see if squirrels had left any acorns underneath. There were quite a few deep cups with the acorns gone, and Aaron picked up two that were fastened together like Siamese twins.

That was his prize to carry home to show Mommy. The fact that they were deep cups, hence from a black oak, escaped him completely. He showed Mommy his "corn" when we got back, and with a little prompting, Peter explained that his two-needle cluster was from a red pine.

❧❧❧

When I was a romantic teenager, I considered the pine my favorite tree. Somehow our southern Wisconsin oak woods came out second best to the magnificent pine forests up north.

Several decades of living among oaks, however, have now inspired me to put them in first place. There is more variety in an oak woods. Two or three trunks may come from one root, leaning politely away to give each other breathing space. The branches spread wide over the edge of the meadow, turning in unexpected graceful shapes. Pine trunks and branches are by contrast rather straight and uninteresting.

Pines don't shed their green annually, either, to open up the view and enlarge our world. Oaks not only oblige us in this fashion, but just before the cold and snow their leaves burst into burnished reds and oranges, intensified on a sunny fall day.

Oaks are a little stubborn, though. They don't lose all their leaves in fall. Just enough so we can enjoy sunsets over Ferry Bluff and sunrises over Blackhawk Ridge. And some years they refuse to turn into bright colors; they stay green until the last possible moment and then turn an uninteresting brown. But the left-behind-for-winter leaves curl up into quaint shapes, rattling companionably in the wind when the rest of the meadow has settled into winter silence. Later they catch snow or ice and make striking patterns against the sky on frosty mornings.

One fall day I started for the garden to gather the last of our tomatoes, but my feet took me out into the meadow and adjacent wildlife refuge, collecting oak leaves instead. Large oaks were still green, but the scrub oak out there displayed leaves in every shade of red from scarlet to mahogany. Some were partly yellow, green or brown.

Several times I have tried to capture and take home this beauty, but never really succeeded. To keep the colors from fading I dipped the leaves in a thin coat of paraffin, or ironed them between sheets of waxed paper. Once I tried to make place mats, laying the leaves artistically on plain white cardboard and covering them with a sheet of clear contact paper. Not successful either.

What happened to the vibrant colors I saw out in the meadow? Dulled by the contact paper? Or are they like all wild things — not meant to be tamed and brought in the house? Maybe those colors are something we should carry in our heads, to be remembered fondly in black, white and gray winter days.

❄❄❄

"Look at that!" I said to Norm as we walked along the upper river path one fall day. "Those have to be oak leaves, but they have rounded lobes, like white oaks. I was sure we had only one kind of oaks here, black." I pointed to a sapling about fifteen feet high.

"These lobes are shallower than those of the white oak," Norm observed.

We waited for the promised visit of our county forester for an answer to our question. His identification was immediate. "Swamp white oak. The leaf is actually kite-shaped. Notice that it's hairy underneath."

In the next few days, I found several small saplings with the same leaves, all fairly close to the river. On a weekend walk through the bottomland along the dike road with Kristin I found some of the mature trees. "There's a swamp white oak," I announced, "and look how big that tree is! It's just as awe-inspiring as a mature burr oak."

We checked the leaves and also brought home some empty acorn cups, one of them a double. According to my tree guide, swamp white oak acorns are often borne in pairs: "scaly, somewhat ridged cup, enclosing lower third of the inch-long acorns." Right on. The bark of the tree is coarsely ridged, almost like a cottonwood.

"Maybe we should clear out the scrub oak and cedars that are crowding out the two best specimens of our swamp white oak," I suggested. "If they grow this well, they will make great eagle-perching trees for our grandchildren to enjoy."

❄❄❄

"I'm sure elves live in that tree," I told Norm as we approached an ancient burr oak on our favorite walk, across the road in the Mazomanie Unit of the Lower Wisconsin Riverway. "Look at all those nooks and crannies."

"That tree was half dead when we first took this walk, twenty years ago," observed Norm. "I don't think it's had any leaves for two or three years." The skeleton of the tree was a weathered silvery gray. Plants wither and animals disintegrate, as Edwin Way Teale points out, but a tree remains "arresting, full of personality."

Passing on, we came to a more open area. Back on the highway, a sign tells us that this is the "Mazomanie Oak Barrens, a Wisconsin State Natural Area." It goes on to explain that except for the young oaks that keep trying to fill the empty spaces, this is the way the land looked when the first settlers came: grasses, wild flowers and an occasional large oak that had escaped prairie fires.

These fires were ignited by lightning, or had been deliberately started by Native Americans to control underbrush. According to early records, settlers also were known to start fires. They burned off old dead grass to encourage the growth of fresh pasture for cattle in spring, or to make it easier to plow the land.

"I suppose if you could erase all that scrub oak from the picture and concentrate on those big old trees, you'd see what the land looked like around here two hundred years ago," Norm remarked as we zipped up our jackets and headed back into the wind toward home.

A few days later Norm, Juliana, Richard and I walked along our Spirit Trail with two friends, Jeb and Barb Barzen. As we came up over a little rise of ground, Jeb and Barb said, almost in unison, "'What a beautiful open-grown oak." I looked and there it was. I had walked by it hundreds of times and never appreciated it fully.

"You ought to get all that little stuff out from underneath it," they suggested.

"That looks like a lot of work," said Richard, knowing full well that young muscles would be required to remove all the young oak, cherry and prickly ash. Nevertheless, I decided I would co-opt someone into helping me do just that.

"The trillium and Virginia bluebell that I brought from our house in Madison several years ago aren't doing well under the oak trees behind the sheds. They're being choked out with a lot of undergrowth. I want to transplant them under our open-grown oak."

"This is a perfect place," Juliana chimed in. "They'll get the early sun before the oak leafs out, and then protection in the shade during the heat of summer."

Norm chopped out some of the prickly ash from under the oak in June, and I transplanted the trillium and bluebells. I wanted to move some of the other spring ephemerals but I couldn't find them — the foliage had already died back.

When we returned from a three-week trip in the motorhome that summer, Juliana and Rich said, "We have a surprise for you. It's on the Spirit Trail. See if you can find it."

They had cleared out the rest of the small cherry, birch, oak, whatever, and left the large prairie oak to stand alone. One side of the tree is too close to red pines and is not fully developed, but the bottom branches on the other side stretch out an impressive thirty-

To Thank a River

five to forty feet. The next spring I managed to transplant some bloodroot and spring beauties just as they finished blooming.

As we admired the tree one day I told Juliana, "If it hadn't been for your hard work, we wouldn't even see this oak for what it is. Sometimes to preserve nature we have to change it."

❦❦❦

"Oh, Anne-Marie, don't do that!" a worried father cautioned his three-year-old daughter. She was busy peeling off the tawny- pink "ruffles" on the river birch tree near our front door.

"She was probably trying to tidy things up. That won't hurt the tree," I said. When we came out here to the riverbank the river birch was new to us. With its soft pink-to-orange peeling bark it is a rather feminine-looking tree next to the rough, dark trunks of oaks.

River birches are longer-lived and hence can become larger than the more familiar white birch. The largest one in Wisconsin, near Mauston, has a trunk 181 feet in circumference measured three feet from the ground. As river birches age, the bark becomes dark and fissured. It may grow as a single trunk or in a graceful clump. Leaves are similar to that of the white birch, pointed oval in shape with coarsely toothed margins. Although the river birch can withstand flooding, and we have some in our bottomland, it will also do well on high dry ground. Both kinds of birch have catkins or cones; those of white birch ripen in early fall.

"Why does this tree shed now?" Norm wondered aloud as he swept river birch catkins off the patio for the third time one warm June day. I had an answer.

"I read that's when germination conditions are best, just after flood waters have receded," I told him. "I suppose it's another example of nature's plans for continuation of the species."

❦❦❦

"That big cherry tree half way down the bank blew down in last night's storm," I bewailed one spring morning. "It's been a regular supermarket for the birds every June and July since we've been here!"

"There are plenty of new ones to take its place," Norm said.

"Small comfort," I replied. "It will take a long time for them to grow."

Young cherry trees have smooth bark with little marks that resemble that of a young birch, but the mature bark is different. When I was a guide at the Bethel Horizons Nature Center one of the naturalists once asked a group of fifth graders, "What does that bark look like?"

They were looking at a big cherry tree. One imaginative youngster thought a minute and said "Potato chips." Black, flaky potato chips.

Orioles and rose-breasted grosbeaks used to come and feed their young regularly in my big cherry tree, and most of the seed-eating birds visited sooner or later. I miss them all. My second reason for enjoying cherry trees so much is the fall color. The leaves turn a delicate shade of rose with undertones of yellow, brightening the whole woods. Oaks turn wine color, river birch and ash are yellow, and pines offer their deep green. It's like an intricate tapestry, provided for free every fall.

❧❧❧

"Come down and see my arboretum," Larry Collins invited us one September day. "I have about 120 varieties of trees in my four acres. And you know, this whole thing got started about fifteen years ago, when Norm and I dug up four white pines from your place and planted them down here."

Larry is the pastor of two local churches; but at home, with his tousled hair, worn blue jeans, and faded flannel shirt, he looks more like his other two roles of musician and tree farmer. He taught a class at Grinnell College one summer called "Dendrology and Theology." I'm sure he finds much food for thought as well as material for sermons while working with his trees.

We found two trees in bloom, a hydrangea with inconspicuous white blossoms and a showy blue althea. "That's a member of the hibiscus family," he told us. "The best time to see my trees is in late spring when more trees are in bloom, like the tamarisk. It has beautiful purple flowers. It likes poor soil, the kind up here around the house."

We walked toward the river to the richer, moister bottomland. "Here's a tree I'm very proud of," Larry said. "That's a bald cypress. They usually grow in swamps down South." His four species of willow thrive there, too: pussy willow, weeping, laurel, and corkscrew. Larry showed us nine species of pine, including Wisconsin's red, white, and jack pines. He also has nine species of oak and nine different kinds of maple trees.

"But here's my special tree," and he pointed at a Korean elder. "It is on loan from the Chicago Botanical Gardens. They wanted to see if it would grow in sandy soil. I suppose they'll want it back some day."

We saw other trees with wonderful names: golden rain tree, smoke tree, yellow wood, yellow horn tree, fern leaf buckthorn and contorted hazelnut.

As we got in the car to leave I told Larry, "At our place we cherish any tree (or plant) that grows on the river bank naturally, especially if it was here in pre-settlement days. But you cherish the ones that don't belong here."

"That's why I have them. It's a challenge to make them survive!" he countered.

"There must be a sermon in there somewhere," Norm called back as he started the car.

❊❊❊

"Those pines all look as though they are dying," said Al Menzer as we canoed the Border Lakes of Minnesota for a week in September. They had a polka-dot look because so many needles were turning orange brown.

"What happened to the pines?" we asked when we got back to the ranger station.

"They look this way every year at this time; pines don't keep their needles forever, any more than deciduous trees do. The difference is they never shed all at once — only a few needles each year," the forest ranger explained.

"Look at those pine needles," said Norm one day. "They are falling and flowing around like our oak leaves do when they come down in the fall." We were in Washington, the Evergreen State, driving through a pine forest on a windy day.

When we arrived home we noticed the polka-dot effect was showing on our own pine trees and I decided to check out the phenomenon.

"You know, the brown needles that are falling off the pines are always several inches back from the end of the branch, so pine branches are bare toward the back. But all the branches on young trees are totally covered with needles," I reported. "So this is a natural, logical process; the healthy green needles are on new growth at the ends of branches." I found that tidbit fascinating, but never found anyone else much impressed.

❊❊❊

"Oh. That's just a common ordinary juniper tree," commented a friend who has some acreage out in the country, a tree farm, actually.

"Yes," I said. *Juniperus virginiana.* Native to our sandy soil. Useful tree — and beautiful, especially in winter when it's covered with tiny blue berries." But she remained unimpressed.

Junipers at all stages of growth can be found on our property. One of the first things Norm did when we bought the place was to transplant some of the little ones to make a snow fence along the driveway. In a few years they were high enough to save him some backbreaking work with the snow shovel.

More than fifty species of birds feed on cedar berries, according to my tree guide. I get a call or two every fall from someone who has a flock of cedar waxwings feasting on their cedar trees.

I have an old book called *Savor and Flavor* that combines scientific information with folklore. From that book I learn that *Juniper communis* grows in many European countries; that it has medicinal properties; and the berries are used to make gin in Holland and England.

Even my strictly factual field guide to trees and shrubs informs me the aromatic heartwood is used for practical things like cedar chests and fence posts, and oil from the leaves is used in perfumes.

So there, my unconvinced friend.

❦❦❦

"You have a nice stand of staghorn sumac here," Wayne Pauly, the county forester, pointed out as he walked our acreage with us one fall day. "With the sun coming through you can see how hairy the branches are — like a stag's antlers in velvet."

We had never noticed this before, but now observed that the other species of sumac has perfectly smooth stems.

What is more glorious in September than a patch of sumac? Its compound leaves, which can have anywhere from seven to thirteen leaflets, are among the first to turn color. And what color! Coral, orange, scarlet, crimson, burgundy, maroon, purple — any or all are possible.

When serving as a guide at the Nature Center I stop at the sumac and ask the children "What are those red velvety things?" They usually answer, "Fruits! And the birds eat them."

But when I say "The Indians used to soak the fruits in water to make a lemonade type of drink," the response is often "Yuck!"

❦❦❦

"Look what a beautiful golden color the mulberry leaves are," I commented at breakfast on the morning after the first hard frost.

A few hours later Norm came in from raking oak leaves to shed his old plaid jacket. "It's getting warm out there. And look at the mulberry tree now. All of a sudden those leaves all came down, and there's not a bit of wind!"

"And look at the ground under the tree — it's the same color the tree was," I responded. "I wonder why they came down all at once?"

Kristin was here, and she immediately volunteered an explanation. "There is a layer of cells between the leaf petiole and the tree branch. Usually each leaf chooses its own time to activate this abscission layer, but the mulberry must be somehow synchronized. One of

To Thank a River 97

the branches still has green leaves. I wonder if they will fall?"

I have kept a journal ever since we moved here, and after a little searching, I found an entry for October 8, 1987: "Another hard frost last night. Twenty-two degrees this morning, and the mulberry leaves were outlined with frost. When the sun hit, they began dropping all at once, although there was no wind. Not all came down, though."

So, were the falling mulberry leaves triggered by the sun, the hard frost, by the exact color they had attained? It would take a lot more records than two to prove anything.

"Research must be boring,," I decided. "I'd rather just enjoy what happens each day and not bother about why it happened."

❅❅❅

Rusty oaks, tawny ash trees, and golden cherry trees now line the river bank. "I never can remember exactly why leaves turn color," I remarked to Kristin. Of course, she was ready with an answer.

"The colors were in the leaves all along, but the green chlorophyll dominated during the growing season. The pigment is in plastids within each cell — they're like little plastic bags. In a microscope you can see the color right through them. In the fall the green plastids decompose, but the other colors last longer."

"But why do they decompose?" I wanted to know.

"Different factors. With some the cause is light; days get shorter, the intensity of the sun is less. With others, a change of temperature, or a lack of moisture."

"If the process is that complicated, no wonder they used to tell us Jack Frost made the leaves turn color," I told her.

❅❅❅

"I have a seed for you to identify," Roger Winans told me one day. "My neighbor Merton Moely found it on a tall shrub at Ferry Bluff."

He gave me a thin, papery thing shaped like a Chinese lantern that rattled when shaken. Merton hadn't seen what kind of leaves the tree had, so I didn't have much more in the way of clues. But I always like a challenge, so I took it home to see what I could determine from my *Field Guide to Trees and Shrubs.*

These guides are divided into sections such as "opposite compound leaves" and I had no idea where to start. So I just paged through, looking at illustrations of seeds and fruits. Surprisingly, after going through almost the whole book, I found a picture that looked exactly like what I was holding in my hand.

"Fruits (are) inflated papery capsules, one to two inches." No question about that, especially when I read on: "No other woody shrub has such fruits." The tree is called bladdernut, which seems

98 *Clausen*

logical enough, and it thrives in bottomland.

I called the Moelys to find out more. "Merton found that seed on a tree close to the river at the end of the road," Mrs. Moely told me. "He tied a string around the trunk so we could find the tree in the spring. We were wondering what kind of leaves and blossoms it would have. But it's nice to know the name."

Just like the face of a stranger that you see often, I thought, when you finally have a chance to meet and find out his name, you have a new friend.

❊❊❊

"Do you know of any tree that blooms in the fall?" It was Joanne Huerth on the phone on an October afternoon. She and her husband have a farm on the other side of the river. "My husband brought home a branch from a small tree that has red flowers on it."

"The only thing I can think of that blooms in the fall is witch hazel," I replied, "but those flowers are very small and sort of greenish."

"Why don't I bring it over, so you can take a look," she suggested.

Very conveniently Kristin was here, and she straightened us out on one point immediately. "This doesn't have any flower parts — no stamens or pistil." She opened one of the little star-shaped capsules and found seeds. "It's the fruit of something, but I've never seen anything like it around here."

We checked all my tree and shrub guides without success, and concluded it must be an ornamental from someone's yard, seed carried by a bird and planted in just the right location for it to thrive.

Several weeks later when we were visiting the Menzers in northern Illinois, Al asked "Would you like a wahoo tree to take home?"

"What's that?" we asked in return. "Is it native to our area?" Al knows we are trying to restore native species when we can.

"Just look out the window. I didn't plant that one. Apparently the tree just grew there in my little oak woods," he said.

"Look at that — star-shaped red berries hanging in clusters. That's the same thing Joanne Huerth brought over a while ago," I told Norm.

"Sure," Norm said, "We'd like to get a little tree in the spring, at the right time for transplanting."

Al had a tree guide in which wahoo was listed, but the tree's range barely reaches into southern Wisconsin. "I wonder how it got that name," I mused.

"Probably because they are so rare you're supposed to say 'WA-HOO' when you see one" Al's suggested.

To Thank a River

❦❦❦

"Have you noticed what's happening to one of those big oaks over by the horseshoe court?" I asked Norm one warm summer day.

"Most of the leaves have died. I suppose its twin will go, too," he replied gloomily.

It's hard to watch a tree die. Especially if it has been shading your house for the last twenty years. When we added the sun room on the southwest side of the house, with windows on three sides, we weren't counting on losing the shade that made it so livable on hot summer days.

"Well, it's gone," Norm observed in September. Every leaf was a lifeless brown.

"I hope you're not going to take it down yourself," I said promptly. Norm loves to make wood, which is local terminology for transforming a dead tree into firewood. I always worry until I know the tree he's working on is safely on the ground.

"No," he assured me, "it's too close to the house. We'll have a professional come. And while he's here, he better take down those three dead trees hanging over the driveway."

"Oh, yes. Every time there's a windstorm I'm afraid we're going to be imprisoned behind a big tree trunk."

Since we are part of the Lower Wisconsin Riverway, the county forester had to come and certify that the trees were dead. We are all in favor of the Riverway objective, to keep the river in a "natural state," but it does restrict the landowner's ability to do anything he wishes on his own property.

The most common cause for dying oaks is oak wilt, but the forester found other trees that were doomed because of chestnut borer. Twenty trees in all would have to go. We'd lost trees before; when you have twenty-five acres, it doesn't seem so bad.

"I'm glad to be rid of the ones along the driveway, but I don't like to lose the ones hanging over the sheds," I told Norm. "I like the pattern of bare branches against the sky, and it's easier to identify birds perching there. No leaves in the way."

The saddest day was when the heavy equipment was actually working in the yard. It was marvelous, of course. Compared to my worries when Norm is working alone, the crew was like a miracle. We watched the little bobcat with a big fork in front neatly carrying away big logs and bunches of branches.

"That's great — saves us from some backbreaking work," we agreed.

But it was noisy, and that big double tree was going down. That was where the oriole nest had been, on the long branch that hung out over the river bank. Not to mention that I used the trunk to anchor my clothes line.

At one time Kristin worked in a research lab in climatology where they counted a lot of tree rings to determine wet and dry seasons in the past (among other things). She came out and looked at several of the big old stumps.

"I found the close-together rings of the 1930s drought," she reported. "Our big double tree must have been about eighty years old."

It will take a long time to grow a tree of that magnificence again, I thought to myself.

XII.
The prairie

An old Dodge came down the long driveway on a lazy summer afternoon. Our house is not visible from the road, and we don't often have unexpected visitors, so I walked out on the porch to greet the elderly man getting out of the car.

"My uncle owned this place once and I just wanted to see what it looks like now," he explained. "It was before they put the dam in, and I used to have to drive the cows across the river to pasture when the water was low enough," he went on. "The only problem was when one of 'em had a new calf on the other side and didn't come back. Then I had to go over and find her and bring 'em both back across the bridge. A long walk."

In answer to my question, he said, "Oh, my uncle stayed here for a while, but the soil was too sandy. He gave up and moved to Canada."

Two hundred years ago, this area consisted largely of oak openings and prairies. It is thought that fires, either accidental or planned by Indians, kept other vegetation from coming in. Oak openings consisted of ten to twelve burr oaks to the acre. These trees have a cork-like bark which is fire-resistant.

Seeing beautiful tall grasses and flowering plants in the prairie, settlers thought they had found very fertile soil. It was — but only for the right kind of plants. Dry, sandy areas like ours will grow only limited species, and does not do much for corn and wheat. Although

102   *Clausen*

grazing and attempts at farming destroyed the lush prairie growth, some of it is returning.

❧❧❧

"This is my restoring prairie," I usually say to visitors taking the obligatory walk that goes with every invitation to lunch or dinner at our house. "Sort of like a recovering alcoholic. My prairie will probably always be restoring."

"See how tall this big bluestem is?" I demonstrate by pointing to clumps higher than my head. "It's also called turkey foot, because of the way the seed head branches into three long parts like a turkey's foot. Switch grass is almost as tall, but it has many dainty seedheads."

As we return to the house, I call attention to the sun coming through at a low angle giving little bluestem a gossamer appearance, as though the whole field of them might suddenly take off.

When visitors show any real interest, they get a lecture on how various plants can thrive in a dry sandy prairie like ours, without any watering — ever.

"See this plant?" I show them one that has fleshy lance-like leaves with serrated edges, alternately clasping a stem about three feet high. The buds at the top develop into white blossoms, which later become green spiny fruiting balls. "It's called rattlesnake master and it can store water in its fleshy leaves."

"Where did it get that name?" someone is sure to ask.

"Native Americans used it in some form to treat snake bites," I tell them. Then I usually proceed to the next lesson, pointing out a compass plant with its deeply lobed, large, thin leaves.

"See how these leaves point north and south? That way the broad surface avoids exposure to strong southern noonday sun."

Because of their long tap roots, prairie plants are not usually transplanted; it's considered better just to plant seeds. I happened to have a chance to buy a potted compass plant, which managed to survive for several years, producing one of its big yellow blooms the second year, and for a couple of more years before mysteriously disappearing.

Young butterfly weed plants are easier to transplant. Of the two I brought home and planted, only one survived. That one did produce three bright orange flowers one summer, and then it too disappeared. Leathery leaves are this plant's defense against losing moisture. Monarch butterflies are said to lay their eggs on butterfly weed because it contains a substance poisonous to birds, so they will not eat the larvae. Too bad my butterfly weed didn't stay with us!

❧❧❧

Restoring a prairie takes patience and know-how, in equal

To Thank a River   103

amounts. The patience I have — most of the time. I have tried to acquire the know-how by taking several prairie restoration courses from the University Extension, by talking to naturalists, and by reading books and articles.

We've appreciated the thimbleweed, flowering spurge, milkweed, sunflowers, bush clover, dotted mint, evening primrose, wild rose, bird's-foot violet and prairie buttercup. They are all very nice, but not spectacular. One year in August we visited the Avoca Prairie, hip-deep in graceful grasses, nodding butterfly weed, coneflowers. I cherished the puccoon, the goldenrod, the milkweed I already had. But I continued to dream about the butterfly weed, the ballet-dancer coneflower. I collected seeds. Endlessly.

But I wished someone who really knew how would plant the seeds. Finally Kristin volunteered. She spent a whole day, mixing, planting and raking. We watched all summer. We had puccoon, goldenrod, milkweed. We watched the next summer. And the next. Puccoon, goldenrod, milkweed.

The next summer, after the puccoon, and just before the milkweed,

One
Perfect
Pale
Purple
Coneflower.

Patience and know-how is what it takes to restore a prairie. A little know-how and a lot of patience.

❀❀❀

"That looks like cactus!" Norm and I said to each other as we took one of our first walks of exploration around the open, sandy area. It was still winter, and the cactus looked lifeless, old and wrinkled. But a few months later, those same fleshy leaves were rejuvenated. They became green and business-like; in June they pushed out spiny buds, and late that month they were covered with rose-like flowers. The petals were a transparent yellow shading to soft orange at the center, perfectly setting off a bouquet of yellow stamens. They looked like tissue paper flowers at a church bazaar.

A few weeks later, each blossom turned into an edible pear, quite delicious if you could eat it without encountering the spines. Perhaps, if horses could manage that, they'd have eaten up our cactus, as well as the other prairie flowers. Horses grazed here until two years before we came. They must have given the cactus a wide berth as they munched their way about; in the sandier open spots we find patches as large as four feet across.

104   Clausen

Each year we begin to see more of the old dry prairie plants returning. June brings one of my favorites, big patches of goat's-rue, looking like a wild sweet pea with its pale yellow and pink blossoms. On a July visit, Jeb Barzen pointed out something special.

"You've got some fame flower here. It's a threatened species in Wisconsin."

He showed us a plant with tiny deep-pink flowers emerging from an almost invisible stem, with a clump of fleshy, needle-shaped leaves at the base. I must be very watchful to see it at all; it's inconspicuous except for the brief period of bloom. As far as I know, it's my only rare plant.

❧❧❧

"What do you suppose this is?" the shorts-clad visitor asked as she headed for the kitchen sink. "And I need a drink of water. It's hot out there." She had picked a tall spike covered with buds. The lowest ones were a light green, becoming raspberry red as they appeared to be climbing upward.

"Gayfeather, blazing star, liatris. Call it any one of the three," I replied. "It will have vivid lavender blossoms, and the odd thing is they bloom from the top down."

"What does it look like when it blooms?" she asked, plopping down on the porch with her glass of water.

"Those flower heads are densely packed with tiny five-pointed stars," I told her, "and each one has two dainty stamens half an inch long. Looks sort of whimsical. It reminds me of the hats the Queen Mother in England wears."

❧❧❧

"Come on, Sadie," I called to our springer spaniel. "There's a cat coming up the path!" We're a little paranoid about cats when there are so many baby birds around. The cat disappeared long before the dog knew why we were there; but now that the cat knows that a dog lives here, she may not return.

On our way back to supper on the porch, something bright and showy caught my eye — a stalk almost three feet tall with lovely lavender blossoms. I couldn't believe my eyes at first because so far my prairie plants had been rather inconspicuous. This one looked as though it belonged in someone's carefully tended flower garden.

I convinced Norm to come out and look at it. "It's so spectacular, it should be easy to identify," I told him.

The flowers were tubular, more than an inch long, with five uneven lobes. The down-turned lobes had purple and white lines leading directly into the throat of the blossom — presumably to guide insects in for pollination. Hanging right over the middle of this "road" was an orange tufted stamen. I counted seven blossoms and at least thirty buds climbing the top half of the stem.

I found, however, that identification wasn't that easy. Nothing quite fit as I paged through my flower guides. I perused notes I had made when I planted seeds in the prairie. There I saw a name that rang a bell — beardtongue. What was beardtongue?

Some of my seed was from the Prairie Nursery at Westfield. I looked through their catalogue, which is illustrated in living color — and there it was. Its scientific name is *penstemon grandiflora,* called beardtongue because of that one tufted stamen in its throat.

The nursery seed had been planted three years earlier, and the following year I had added some beardtongue seed that Donald Kindschi gave me. So that beardtongue took two or three years to appear. Over a period of eight years we sowed the seed of over thirty different prairie forbs and several grasses. All the grasses are accounted for, but only seven flower species besides the beardtongue have appeared. I wonder how many years it will take the rest to blossom?

***

"You're going to burn your prairie? Aren't you afraid you'll catch your woods on fire?" This is sometimes the reaction when I mention this phase of prairie maintenance. I suppose it does conjure up pictures of flames high in the air with people scurrying to protect their property. But it's not like that at all.

"Indians and even some of the first settlers used to burn regularly to keep their prairies healthy," I usually explain. "This little prairie would be filled with things like honeysuckle, aspen, and prickly ash if we didn't burn it every few years. Nature abhors a vacuum."

We also have a lot of non-native bromegrass that doesn't like to share space with the turkeyfoot, little bluestem, and Indian grass we are trying to encourage. The bromegrass comes up first, and the fire sets it back, while the warm open soil stimulates the growth of true prairie grasses and forbs.

Jeb and Barb Barzen have formed a prairie burning service. One fine April day they gathered together at our place a crew of eight people, not counting me. I was in charge of picture-taking and the coffee break.

Jeb began assigning tasks. "Rich, you get the hoses hooked up so we can fill our water tanks. Jean, you call your neighbors and alert them we're doing a controlled burn so they won't be worried. Juliana, you have the burn permit don't you?"

Jeb consulted a little gadget that measured humidity, then went

106   Clausen

in the house and phoned the weather bureau to check wind velocity and direction. At last all seemed to be ready.

"Juliana, Rich, Jeff — who else wants to wear an eight-gallon water tank on your back? They weigh forty pounds." Jeb made more assignments. Barb was excluded from this job because she was eight months pregnant at the time of our first burn. She and Bev carried small tanks of a flammable liquid called flame drippers.

"The rest of you take these flappers," Jeb concluded. Flappers were long poles with squares of rubber on the end with which to beat out any unwanted flames.

However, there weren't many unwanted flames. Half the crew went to the end of the intended burn against the way the wind was blowing, and started a line of fire there. It burned slowly and soon burned out, thus forming a natural barrier for the main fire which would go with the wind. Of course, an extremely windy day would not have been chosen; the flames never got very high or moved very fast. You do have to have some wind, though, or the process would take too long.

As the crew left, they admired the velvet blackness of land sloping toward the pines. Two weeks later it was brilliant green.

❧❧❧

In a couple of months Jeb came back to evaluate results. I had already noticed how many more brassy yellow clumps of puccoon could be seen in the burned area.

"That bromegrass is sparser and shorter where we burned," Jeb said as we stood at the edge of the East Meadow.

"I found four beardtongues this year," I told him proudly, as we started down the path. "They had about a dozen blossoms each."

"Your rattlesnake master looks very healthy," commented Jeb, wading into the deeper grasses. "And so does the new one that just came up last year."

"I had a compass plant in here somewhere, but it hasn't come up for two years," I told him.

"There it is!" he said. After examining it closely, he decided it probably wouldn't bloom until next year.

"Fifteen buds on the pale purple coneflower," I said, counting as we walked toward the river. "It had only six blossoms last year. And this must be another prairie flower, but I don't know what it's going to be."

"That's showy goldenrod," he replied, "a beautiful flower." I was delighted. I've been waiting six or seven years for that to come up.

"I see the fire killed some of the small cherry trees," Jeb ob-

To Thank a River 107

served.

"I wish it would take care of more of those little oaks," I complained. The hardest part of maintaining a prairie is keeping trees from encroaching. But all in all, I was very happy with the results of our first professional burn.

❄❄❄

"Notice how the prairie flowers are mostly yellow in August?" I asked Norm one day. "It was all blues and pinks a month ago."

"I see goldenrod is beginning to bloom," he acknowledged.

"And sunflowers, and brown-eyed Susan — even butter'n'eggs, where the grasses give them a chance," I pointed out.

Rusty heads of Indian grass and purplish turkeyfoot tower over everything else. Columns of broad milkweed leaves provide contrast in shape and texture. As I wandered around admiring it all one day I noticed another spot of yellow.

"Something's new out there that doesn't look like anything from a seed we planted," I reported to Norm, who was deep in the morning paper. "I wonder where it could have come from, and what it is."

The plant was only a foot or two high, but its finely cut compound leaves were almost as eye-catching as the bright yellow flowers. Tucked into leaf axils, the blossoms were about a half inch across with five unequal broad petals centered by dark red drooping anthers.

The leaves reminded me of leadplant and goat's rue, so I looked them up in my flower guide. I soon found that these two belong to the rather large bean family; most of those have seeds that are borne in pods. But my new flower wasn't among them.

On the same pages as the bean family I found the senna family, with two members in our region. First was wild senna which had similar leaves, but the flower looked more like goldenrod. The second was my new discovery without a doubt: "partridge pea, blooms July to September; dry meadows and prairies, inland sands."

So that's where it came from; it wasn't spontaneous generation (which back in the Dark Ages was actually thought to be possible), but a seed hidden in sandy soil just waiting for the right conditions to develop. We plant seeds and sometimes wait years for them to come up. In the meantime nature keeps us encouraged by providing delightful surprises like partridge pea.

❄❄❄

"There's something scratchy along the bottom of my blue jeans,"

108 Clausen

I told Norm as I came in from a walk one September day.

"Probably a sand burr. Pull it off and burn it. We don't need any more of those!" And he returned to his golf magazine.

"No, look at this," I persisted. "It's a long narrow seedhead ending in three *awns,* like fine wire. They twist around each other and then spread out like a three-blade propeller. No wonder it felt scratchy."

We are used to "hitchhikers" this time of year, trying to get themselves planted as far as possible from their parents. A prairie grass guide book informed me this one was triple-awn grass. When they've reached a place they like, apparently they uncurl and plant the seed. The next day I retraced my steps and found triple-awn grass growing along a fence row. It is only a foot or so high and not very spectacular looking; no wonder it has to hitchhike to get attention.

❧❧❧

Our thermometer registered one degree below zero on a frosty January morning. "That's the largest flocked Christmas tree I've ever seen," I said to Norm.

The big white pine stood in the middle of the East Meadow, its needles rich with hoarfrost.

Fog covered the river and hoarfrost decorated every leaf and twig. A new sound caught my ear — the loud *sh-sh-sh* of sheets of ice hurrying downstream with the current, rubbing against ice imprisoned on shore. The sun, still low in the east, sent uncertain rays through fog. Beyond the meadow, slender oaks and aspens peeked through the mist, like young girls too shy to join the party.

Even the lowly red cedar, or juniper, was special with its share of frosty embellishment. Curled-up oak leaves, scarcely noticed yesterday, were eye-catching, their rich brown contours outlined in furry white.

When I passed here the other day, last summer's goldenrod was dingy and brown. Today it was reincarnated in ethereal white, its drooping heads even more graceful than the stiffer blooms of fall. Bush clover still stood straight and proud, because it lasts two years before it crumbles into nothingness. Next fall, when new plants are soft and brown, these will be graying and shedding seeds.

Here and there a clump of little bluestem fanned out from shallow snow in a graceful arc, its stem ends uninteresting now that the gossamer seedheads are gone. Wild rye bowed its head deeply, but each empty seedhead stood out clearly. Seedless switch grass reinforced with hoarfrost made a dainty pattern against the blue river behind it.

As I returned to the house the lawn was a sterile sheet of clean white snow. Behind me prairie grasses in the meadow rose from their tawny beds as ghostly, larger-than-life images of their summer selves. The superiority of a natural prairie over a short-cropped lawn was never more clearly demonstrated.

XIII. Animals

"Is someone still camping across the river?" I asked Norm one Monday morning at breakfast.

"That does look like a child and a dog," he replied. We both reached for binoculars.

What we actually saw were three deer exploring the sandy shore, sniffing at the scent left by yesterday's human occupants. Early morning sun brought out the tawny color of their fur, and their every movement was pure grace. One or the other of the three constantly had his head up and on the alert, turning in every direction like radar to sense danger.

They explored the area and the undergrowth nearby, stopping often to pose like statues on a lawn. Finally they raised their white tails and loped slowly off into the woods, seemingly convinced that it was theirs once again to enjoy with only their natural neighbors.

We see more animal signs than animals — little raccoon tracks down on the swimming beach, or deer tracks along the Spirit Trail. Sometimes in the fall, when grasses get long, we find big squashed-down places where we assume deer have slept the previous night. Occasionally we see the deer itself slipping through the woods or across the meadow on its way to the river for a drink. Each glimpse is treasured.

"What's that I hear?" asked Norm one dark, soft night in early summer. A loud melodious song or call, a sustained trill, it seemed to be coming from the trees.

"Tree frogs!" I hazarded a guess, but we couldn't see any. Listening to our frog-calling tape proved me right. Later that summer we met a tree frog several times.

In late afternoon when the sun begins to come in the front windows we let the awnings down. A two-inch-long tree frog often uses the deep fold of the awning as a pleasant place to sleep away daylight hours.

He finds it pleasant, that is, until his protection vanishes and hot afternoon sun begins to dry out his comfortably moist skin. Usually undisturbed, he blinks drowsily, then eventually hops away to find a shady spot to continue his day's sleep.

"Watch when I let the awnings down!" I told our visiting ten-year-old grandson Peter one hot summer day. As usual, a tree frog fell out, and of course Peter picked it up immediately. It did not seem averse to being carried about and admired for a short time. Peter placed the tree frog on the window, then went inside.

"Look at those suction cups just behind his toes," said Peter. "So that's how he can climb trees!"

"And houses, windows and awnings," I added.

I got out one of my reference books and turned to tree frogs. "Turn him over and see what color the back of his hind thigh is," I suggested to Peter.

Peter carefully turned him over. "Yellow and black," he replied.

"Gray tree frog," I said. "It says here that their most conspicuous field mark is that the inner surface of the hind thigh is bright yellow or orange mottled with black. He's gray all right, but the picture in my book shows more of a green color."

The next afternoon Peter was ready when we opened the awning. "He's green!" he reported.

"Must have been clinging to a green stripe," I suggested. "They change color to blend with their environment, but the transformation can take as much as an hour."

The main color in our awning is brick red — and sure enough, for the next two days our tree frog chose that spot for his bed and developed a definite reddish hue by the time we disturbed his sleep.

"I wonder where he goes in the winter?" Peter asked.

Back to the reference book. We learned that all frogs spend the winter in aquatic vegetation at the bottom of some body of water. Even though they breathe through their lungs the rest of the year, in hibernation they breathe through their skin.

"Frogs are valuable," I told Peter. "They eat flies and other insect pests. I hope he lives a long time."

In turn, they provide food for game fish, shore birds and ducks. They are an important part of the food chain.

"Do you think this tree frog will ever decide it's better to sleep in a tree than to get dumped out of the awning every day?" Peter asked.

❊❊❊

"There's a bat in here!" is usually a signal to persons sitting on our screened porch to quickly shut the door to the house, then open both porch doors until the bat leaves. In the meantime conversations go on as usual. Unless a visitor says "Aren't you afraid the bat will get in your hair?"

"Bats are not blind," Richard patiently explains. (His bachelor's degree is in biology.) "They use an intricate sonar system to avoid obstacles and to catch their prey. They send out high frequency sounds that bounce off solid objects, and the bats can interpret the echoes. They're not interested in a woman's hairdo or anything as solid as a human being. Bats are only interested in insects."

A single bat may eat one-fourth to one-third of its body weight in a single night. For many years, Europeans have erected bat houses in their back yards and in their national forests to control the insect population.

When we let down the awnings on a hot summer afternoon, the surprise that drops out is sometimes a little brown bat. I always enjoy this opportunity to examine more closely one of these night creatures. The bat is mouse-size, with soft brown fur. (It looks soft; I haven't tried touching it!) The German word for bat is *Fledermaus,* which means flying mouse. Like the mouse, the bat is a mammal, gives live birth, and nurses its young — usually one to each mother per year.

After my little bat's slumber has been interrupted, he rests a moment, then spread his "arms" and flies off to a tree to await the proper time for his activities. Bats are unique among mammals — the only ones to achieve true flight. Their wings are constructed similarly to human arms, the wings being greatly elongated "fingers" covered with a thin membrane.

Bats are the most misunderstood and unjustly maligned of nature's creatures, according to Merlin Tuttle, a leading bat researcher and curator of the Milwaukee Public Museum. Myths have been perpetrated by the press, the movies, and fiction writers until most people believe them.

I sometimes think that bats also have a sense of humor, at least the ones who lived in the belfry of our church one summer. Otherwise why would one of them wake up just in time for the sermon and make several forays around the sanctuary, often just above the heads of the congregation? I think they enjoy seeing people duck — the ones who don't know about the bats' sophisticated sonar system.

❊❊❊

Spider season! I thought as I carefully picked up a daddy long-legs by two legs and carried him outside. Any other spider that invades my domain is unmercifully crushed. "Now why didn't I crush the daddy-long-legs?" I asked myself.

Evidently I believed someone long ago who told me that kind of spider didn't bite, that it was in fact beneficial to humans. I decided to find out if there was any scientific basis for this belief. A trip to the library yielded more than I really wanted to know about spiders.

I was aware, of course, that they were not insects; insects have six legs and spiders eight. But I didn't know that daddy longlegs are not true spiders. Spiders are *Arachnida araneae,* and daddy longlegs (also called harvestmen) are *Arachnida opiliones.* The main visible difference is that spiders have a waistline and daddy longlegs don't.

About the only thing I didn't want to learn was that spiders are misunderstood and most are beneficial. But I was intrigued by daddy longlegs. My long-ago informant was right; they don't bite, and they do eat living insects, such as mites, spiders, caterpillars, and centipedes.

One important thing I learned was that I should be more careful about which two legs I pick him up by. The second pair of legs, usually waving about in the air, is covered with very fine hairs, which are its "ears." At the tips of this pair of legs are some dark patches which are for smelling and tasting. Without these legs, the spider would have a difficult time finding food and might even become disoriented.

Daddy longlegs have eyes on top of the body, one facing right and one left, giving them almost 360-degree vision. Except for sight, all their other senses are in the legs. Each leg has coarse hairs which are used for the sense of touch. The legs end in small claws, enabling him to run lightly along the top of grass, instead of on the ground around it.

The next time I find a daddy longlegs, I want to get better acquainted before I escort him out.

❊❊❊

"Look at this spider!" said Tom, one of the friends Juliana and I were chatting with at Indian Lake County Park on an idyllic fall day.

"What kind is it?" I asked.

"I don't know, but isn't it beautiful?" he answered.

114   Clausen

About the size of a grape, it was black with an interesting yellow pattern on the body. Tom let it crawl around on his hand long enough for us to admire it, then set it free in the long grass where it wouldn't be stepped on.

I wondered privately if it was poisonous, but it showed no interest in biting, only in getting away. Back at the library the next day, I learned that this was a female garden spider, the species that we are most likely to find. (Not poisonous.) If it had been a male, he would have been much smaller.

Early on a dewy morning, I read, you might find a two-foot-square garden spider web spun between tall plants. If a fly strikes the web, the spider goes into frenzied activity. Picking up the insect, she turns it constantly, wrapping it tightly in silk spun from her spinnerets. This takes only seconds. She then inflicts a fatal bite. If the insect were a grasshopper, the wrapping process would take longer, about a minute. The prey may be eaten immediately or left to hang a while.

I began to wonder where spiders spend the winter. If I can believe the video *Charlotte's Web,* which I watched with my grandchildren on a summer visit, spiders don't spend the winter anywhere; they die. But their eggs are neatly tied up in a little sack of silk, and baby spiders emerge when the time is right in spring.

I had read once again that very few spiders are poisonous or will bite humans, and they all destroy insect pests. I suppose I should appreciate all spiders more... Well, maybe.

❈❈❈

An insistent bark from our dog, Sadie, called me from my work in the garden on an early summer day. Since she seldom barks, I went to investigate. It was a stand-off. Sadie stood with her head lowered and feet firmly planted, glowering at something about three feet away. A snake, three or four feet long, was coiled in the grass with his head raised, sticking his tongue out and hissing at her.

The snake looked quite handsome there in the lush grass. He was yellowish, with large dark brown spots marching in neat rows along his back and sides.

"Come here, Sadie," I said. She seemed relieved to retreat. I think she was afraid, only standing her ground as a matter of duty. I knew it couldn't be a rattler, but I called the dog off anyway; I didn't want her to hurt the snake.

Investigation showed that Sadie had found a fox snake, also called a pine snake, and that they have a particular appetite for rodents. I hope he lives, prospers, and has many children. I also hope he got

To Thank a River

the mouse that entered my closet last summer and decided that my favorite sweater would make good nesting material.

"There's a chipmunk!" a visitor will often say, when looking out at our bird feeding area.

"That's not a chipmunk, it's a thirteen-line ground squirrel," I usually reply without even looking up. I've never seen a chipmunk here. The two animals are certainly similar, but ground squirrels are more streamlined, with small ears and large eyes.

Although our ground squirrels never sit still long enough for me to check if there are exactly thirteen stripes down their backs, I do admire the color scheme. The stripes alternate, buff colored and deep brown, with yellowish spots.

We enjoy watching ground squirrels dart about the yard looking for tender shoots of weeds and grasses. When they find something to their liking, they sit bolt upright to eat it out of their paws.

Jackson's *Mammals of Wisconsin* tells me ground squirrels spend the winter in burrows which they dig themselves. Their body temperature may go down as low as thirty-three degrees, while heart beat and breathing slow to once or twice a minute. The burrow is a tunnel, twelve to fifteen feet long and six to twelve inches under the surface. A cavity in the burrow about eight inches in diameter is lined with dry grass and leaves and used for nesting.

About July somebody usually notices "those cute little baby ground squirrels," already big enough to hunt for tender shoots to eat. By September they are fully grown. Early in October they will dig their own burrows and hibernate.

That long tunnel may have been what made it easy for ground squirrels to have their own private entrance to our garden, in spite of a fence. Most of our peas were always neatly nipped off as soon as they got a couple of inches high. Maybe those little varmints aren't so cute after all!

❦❦❦

"Let's sneak up on that turtle!" some child was always saying on our annual Wisconsin River canoe trips. But no matter how quietly they guided the canoe toward a log, at the last moment the wary turtle would slip into the water and disappear.

Looking dull-colored and uninteresting from afar, they failed to arouse my curiosity. Nevertheless, when I saw one walking very slowly across the highway as I was driving home from town one August day, I immediately stopped to rescue it. I'm not sure it appreciated being rescued. The turtle probably would have made it safely to the other side of the road and eventually to the river. Instead it was the subject of intense interest by several adults, and especially by a visiting five-

116   Clausen

year-old named Peter. Not to mention our springer spaniel Sadie.

"Where's the turtle?" I asked after I had gathered some reference materials together.

"Peter and I released it by the river," Kristin answered. "We didn't know you wanted to save it."

When we went down to try to retrieve it, Sadie came to meet us with the turtle in her mouth, unhurt. (After all, springers are supposed to retrieve game.)

We improvised a cage. "I'll get some grass," Peter offered.

"Maybe I can catch some flies for it," said Kristin. The turtle, however, showed interest only in the water pan, but mostly in tipping it over as he struggled to climb out of the improvised cage.

Even the dull olive green back was prettier than it looked from a canoe. Each scute (sort of a platelet) on the carapace (top shell) was outlined faintly in orange.

"Look at the underside of the carapace," I showed Peter.

Where it joins the plastron or bottom shell it was intricately patterned in orange and yellow. The plastron was yellow with an irregularly rectangular dark blotch in the middle.

"Her head is striped with yellow," Kristin noticed.

"Her feet sort of have orange stripes," said Peter.

Painted indeed! But colorful only to the lucky few who can examine one out of its watery habitat.

"Be careful," I warned. "Turtles don't have teeth, but they can bite. They have a sharp ridge along the jaw line and a horny beak. It says here they eat insects, earth worms, and aquatic plants."

Painted turtles nest from May to July, producing one or two clutches a year. The female digs a nest cavity four inches deep in sand or soft earth, and lays anywhere from two to twenty eggs. She carefully covers them and goes off to let sun and the heat of the soil incubate them for about ten weeks. Hatchlings claw their way out. They are very vulnerable to predators, but those that make it can live forty to fifty years. We decided that our turtle was a female, because her plastron was flat; the male's is concave. When we had found out all we really needed to know about painted turtles, we set this one gently in the river itself, and she immediately swam off to freedom.

In October, high water brought a perfect turtle log to rest in full view of our living room windows. On quiet days six, eight, ten, even nineteen turtles could be counted sunning themselves in a neat row.

"Those are map turtles," Richard informed me. "The young have yellow map-like lines on the carapace, but the lines are very faint on adult males and absent on females. See that yellow spot just below the eye, and the ridge running down the middle of the cara-

To Thank a River

pace? That's the easiest way to identify map turtles."

I showed the turtles to a Girl Scout troop who visited on a mild October day.

"We don't want to scare them, but how many can you count?" I asked.

"I count twenty!" several of the girls whispered.

"Can you see the ridge and the yellow eye spot?" I asked. "Now we'll go very quietly down the steps and watch them slide off into the river."

Before we could move, every turtle vanished into the water, in spite of our precautions. We couldn't see that anything had disturbed them down below, either.

Later I read that map turtles are very wary. "The slightest disturbance will send them 'as one' into the water," stated a book by Richard E. Nichols called *The Running Press Book of Turtles*. Most turtles have hard shells which make them almost predator-proof. Only the head, tail and legs protrude from the carapace and plastron. In times of danger they can pull all these appendages safely inside. Because they are tough, adaptable creatures with a unique body design, they have been on this earth for some 450 million years. "Turtles were here before us," states Nichols. "Here, in this world, when the dinosaurs failed and became extinct. And here they have remained."

❧❧❧

One summer evening at dusk I sat on the bench above the swimming beach and watched an adult beaver swimming back and forth. Once he paused to eat some green leaves on a bush close to the water's edge. He finally swam close enough that I could see the broad, flat head and small ears, and the scaly tail shaped like a Ping-pong paddle. When I made a sudden movement he was under the water in an instant, with a loud slap of his tail on the water. It was so loud I understood how it serves as a danger signal for fellow beavers, recognizable for half a mile or more.

"Isn't that a beaver swimming in toward that overhanging box elder tree?" I asked Norm as we were eating an early breakfast a few days later.

"Yes, I've seen him there several times."

Walking along the bank nearby that afternoon, I found a place where some asters and grass had been trampled down, as though an animal had been making a path through them toward the river. Following the path away from the river, I spotted pointed stumps with broad tooth marks, and fresh wood chips with matching tooth marks on the ground. Definitely beaver work.

I know that beavers build dams, but they couldn't be planning to dam the Wisconsin River at a point where it is four hundred feet wide. They must be using the saplings for food; they eat leaves, twigs and bark, stored under water to keep fresh for winter. A week or so later, a few more saplings had disappeared, one a box elder at the spot where we had seen the beaver swimming toward shore.

Mammals of Wisconsin by H.T. Jackson explained that beaver sometimes live in burrows with an underwater entrance. This entrance leads upward into a little room which is dry and warm. All that winter when we looked down at that overhanging tree, we visualized a family of eight or ten beavers living there, safe from predators and unseen by human eyes.

"How do you suppose they anchor their food supply?" I asked. "The current in this river is pretty strong. There must be quite a tangle of tree roots under all that box elder and silver maple; maybe that serves as their winter refrigerator."

"If they can figure out how to build dams to construct ponds to build houses in, I guess they can solve the problem of how to keep their winter's food supply from floating away," said Norm.

❊❊❊

One day while we were skiing in the Mazomanie Wildlife Refuge our springer spaniel suddenly became more purposeful in her hitherto aimless wanderings, evidently trying to follow the fresh scent of some animal.

"There's a possum over there. She's sniffing at the wrong tree," Norm said.

I could see a blob of gray fur comfortably hanging about six feet off the ground in the crotch of a small tree.

"Look here, Sadie!" Norm called.

She obeyed with more alacrity than usual, jumping vainly up on the trunk and clawing with her forepaws as high as she could reach.

The opossum remained unperturbed, his little pointed gray face resting on a branch, long pointed bare tail hanging carelessly curled along the trunk. His eyes were closed. He finally opened them when Norm, much to my consternation, gently nudged the opossum with a ski pole. But the little animal closed his eyes and went on calmly playing possum. I'm sure he knew he had nothing to fear from these humans and that inept dog.

❊❊❊

"What's that little thing under the bird feeder?" I asked Norm one winter morning. "He's fast!"

We were having one of those very snowy winters, and snowbanks surrounding the feeder had grown to about three feet. A small dark

To Thank a River

body about the size of a junco had emerged from a hole in the snowbank, a hole so inconspicuous we weren't aware it was there. This animal scooted around, picking up seeds and holding them in its front paws as it consumed them. It never got very far from the hole, and suddenly, like lightning, it would disappear back into the snowbank.

"It must be a mole, or maybe a vole," Norm guessed.

The tiny critter was kind enough to reappear a couple more times so we could decide whether it was a mole, vole, or shrew. He was chubby, furry, blunt-nosed and four or five inches long, counting his short tail. *Mammals of Wisconsin* came to our rescue again, with pictures of all three animals in question. The short-tailed shrew is about five inches long, but he has a very pointed nose. So does the mole, which is only three inches long.

The only one of these animals that was blunt-nosed was the meadow vole: "stocky and rounded, with little separation between head and body ... ears somewhat obscured by long, soft fur." The description fit. We learned that voles tend to remain beneath the surface, where they travel in snowy tunnels and have their snug nests. In summer they live in tunnels cut through grass, not underground like moles.

"It's amazing what goes on around here that we are not aware of," I remarked as I put away the book and prepared to write my weekly column. About voles, of course.

XIV. Sauntering

"I have met with but one or two persons in the course my life who understand the art of Walking, that is, of taking walks, who had a genius, so to speak, for sauntering..." So states my mentor, Henry David Thoreau. (There must be something about the Wisconsin River; Thoreau was also a mentor for August Derleth.)

I believe Robert Deer was referring to sauntering when he wrote an article in *Wisconsin Natural Resources* a few years ago. Deer is a member of the Menominee tribe, and he describes the spirit trail along the Wolf River: "Our dead never forget the beautiful world that gave them being," he wrote. "They still love its verdant valleys... and often return, to visit, guide, console and comfort us."

Most important to the Menomonie are respect for wildlife, respect for nature, a sense of place for everything in a natural order, and a partnership with nature. When he walks the spirit trail, Deer says, "I hear the voices and rekindle the spirits of those who walked the spirit trail before me."

After I read that article, I quoted Robert Deer in my next column, and ever since then the family has been calling our trail the Spirit Trail. It is about three-fourths of a mile long and goes more or less around the perimeter of our place. The path began as a ski trail many years ago and is now used winter and summer. I can't remember how its exact course was determined. Could it have been a spirit trail of the Sauk tribe? We follow it often and "hear the voices and rekindle the spirits of those who walked before (us)."

When I'm out for exercise, a walk around the Spirit Trail should take about fifteen minutes. Covering the same trail when there are new signs of spring takes about an hour. That's sauntering.

Thoreau has positive ideas about where one's sauntering should be done. "When we walk, we naturally go to the fields and woods: what would become of us, if we walked only in a garden or a mall?" This was written in 1854 — and we thought the mall was a modern invention!

Thoreau believes it is necessary to get into the woods, in spirit as well as in body. "What business have I in the woods if I am thinking of something out of the woods?" I recommend this. Let the mind roam freely, ignoring everything waiting for you back in the house.

❦❦❦

"Do you want to go to Pine Hollow on Mother's Day again this year?" Kristin asked when she telephoned.

"Absolutely!" I answered. Juliana joined us.

As we walked in hot sunlight through the meadow we noted that daisies would soon be in bloom. Entering the woods I remarked, "These leaves are almost full size and they hide the warblers I'm trying to identify. But I do appreciate their shade."

Layers of dead oak leaves made slippery going on the descent to the brook below. Accidentally I learned that sliding on them would be the easiest way to go down. Walking along the stream was not easy either. Mossy boulders and stones of all sizes outline its path through the hollow. Juliana gave me a sturdy straight branch that she found. It was just the right height for a walking stick, and that third leg helped me over the rough spots.

"Get down and look at these closely — it's miterwort," said Kristin. "Look through your binoculars the wrong way; it's like a magnifying glass."

These white flowers climbing up a slender stem above two stalkless leaves are supposed to look like a miter, or bishop's cap; but they are so tiny it's really hard to tell. The earlier ephemerals, now gone, were represented by huge leaves — hepatica, bloodroot, and especially skunk cabbage.

"Lots of jack-in-the-pulpits" reported Juliana, "still in their prime."

"And a few trillium blossoms," I noted. We followed the stream, and came to a little peninsula where another creek joined in.

"This is violet heaven," said Kristin, and she identified four different species, including a dainty yellow one I had never seen before.

We stopped to eat our lunch on a mossy rock, looking off downstream toward shafts of sunlight sifting through maple and hemlock

122 Clausen

trees. The stillness of the forest was enhanced by the gurgling of the brook as it made its way through the narrow valley, and by occasional bird calls. "All these bird songs are familiar, but I haven't heard them since last summer, and it's frustrating to try to sort them out," I complained.

"That sounds like one of the vireos," I finally decided. My bird guide showed that the red-eyed vireo sings short, deliberate phrases, as opposed to the long warbling song of the (what else?) warbling vireo. Red-eyed vireo, probably.

May apples spread their umbrellas everywhere, a bud under some. Eventually we found one that had blossomed, and knelt down to take in the heady perfume.

"That patch of small dark green leaves is trailing arbutus," Kristin pointed out. "There are a few red berries, but the pink flowers are long gone. It's a northern Wisconsin flower, but it grows here in the Pine Hollow microclimate."

Having admired the stately rock wall a bit farther down, we headed back along the brook and up the hill. With the aid of my "third leg," an occasional helping hand from a daughter, and a few rest stops, I made it back to the meadow.

We drove home through more beautiful Sauk County hills and valleys, to pick off our wood ticks and join Norm and Richard, who were grilling bratwurst. A perfect Mother's Day!

❧❧❧

Early one August morning Nancy Appleyard and I sauntered through Walking Iron Park near Mazomanie. Fog was clearing just as we left our car in the parking lot, and every leaf was sparkling and dew-covered.

Literally dozens of spider webs along the pathway claimed our attention.

"Turn around and look at one of those with the sun coming over your shoulder," said Nancy. "The droplets of water are like tiny colored beads."

I began to realize how many different styles of architecture exist in the spider world, since each species spins differently. Some webs were dainty lace doilies; some were intricate houses with domed roofs and different rooms on different levels. Others were hammocks and one was a tiny trampoline.

"I hear an indigo bunting singing from the top of a dead tree across the field," I said. "But he's too far away for us to enjoy his brilliant blue color."

"There's the male in a pine tree just a few feet ahead of us," Nancy said.

"And there's his gray mate," I added. We watched the two of them moving silently among the branches for a few minutes before they disappeared further into the woods.

"What are these prairie plants?" I asked. They were about two feet tall and reminded me of bush clover or thimbleweed, both of which grow in our East Meadow.

"I don't know either," said Nancy, producing a flower guide and looking among the clover pages. She found them both: white prairie clover and purple prairie clover. When the lower half of the flowers are in bloom, tiny green buds protrude above them, like a thimble.

The steep, winding path leading down to a stream and woodland below brought us to a different world of tall oaks, birches, and knee-high ferns. Suddenly we were aware of a tawny red doe, silently watching our approach. We halted abruptly and raised our binoculars. With three long, graceful leaps the doe was almost concealed behind some young maples.

"She's watching something," I said.

"I see something that same tawny color on the path ahead of us," Nancy replied.

Cautiously we walked on, binoculars ready. Rounding a bend we saw a fawn standing in the path about fifty feet away. Through our glasses we saw an expression of gentle curiosity in those big round eyes. We stared at each other intently for a few moments, then the fawn turned and melted into the woods. We didn't see or hear the mother leave.

Although that part of the woods is narrow, with a steep bank on one side and a marsh on the other, we saw no more signs of the deer.

"Probably they are watching us from some hidden vantage point," I suggested.

"Amused at our noisy walk through their woods, with our heavy footsteps snapping twigs," added Nancy.

❀❀❀

September

Come walk with me by the river:
The day is chilly and dull
But soft warmth in moist air
Soon has me shedding my jacket.
I barely miss stepping on
A tiny orange-red fungus.
Suddenly ash trees are golden.
Asters are clouds of blue smoke
Floating beneath the oaks.

Sumac is fire-red.
A large mottled brown bird
Flies above my path
From tall pine into scrub oak.
Only an owl can fly so silently.
Two canoes paddle swiftly
Toward downstream mists.
What will they find
Beyond that diaphanous curtain?

❊❊❊

My favorite time to saunter along the Spirit Trail alone is on a sunny October day. Beyond the tired greens and browns of grasses that were still bright green a month ago, I see that aspens are polka-dotted with yellow. Some of the cherry trees have turned soft yellow tinged with pink. Passing through the pines, I come to large low patches of scarlet sumac which has seemingly changed color overnight. Just beyond are scrub oaks, where every leaf shouts a different color, from orange through reds to mahogany. Their elders, tall sedate oaks near the house, cling tenaciously to summer green.

Frost asters still sprinkle the open areas with white. Sweet everlasting raises grayish cheerful heads in abundance. (One of my naturalist mentors, Ken Lange, calls this cudweed, but my regional flower guide, *Wildflowers and Weeds,* calls it sweet everlasting. That leaves a pleasanter taste as it rolls off the tongue.) I pick a seedhead, crush it in my fingers and am rewarded with a spicy fragrance.

We're not aware of dewberry vines much in their season; birds always manage to get the berries. But in October, dewberry leaves cover the ground with an exuberance of rosy red.

Back in the dryer portion of the meadow I notice the fruits of prickly pear cactus are ripe and red. Carefully picking one I find the fruit delicious, but I eat no more. One of the spines is stuck in the roof of my mouth.

Single stalks of butter-'n'-eggs are scattered like candles under oak trees. Bittersweet vines boast little orange balls, just waiting for something to cause them to open and reveal even brighter orange seeds inside. Would frost be the trigger? I've never been sure.

Warm cinnamon-colored bush clover holds its seed tightly. Last year's stalks stand nearby, dropping their seeds from grayish heads. Culver's root along the bank looks like candelabra; in August the candles were ivory, now wrought iron. Mullein plants, which some people call Indian tobacco, stand like sentinels over the fast-fading goldenrod.

Faint honking in the distance, coming closer, confirms the inevitable; the first skein of geese fly over, methodically making their way south.

❧❧❧

For several weeks after our young springer spaniel, Sadie, became part of our lives, I took a morning walk regularly. Sadie's pleading brown eyes gave walks priority over unmade beds and breakfast dishwashing. A typical fall excursion, half way between a walk and a saunter, would go like this:

Once outside, the early morning world brightens considerably. A shaft of sunlight reaches over Blackhawk Ridge and lights up the rusty, tawny oaks ahead. A moment later it disappears, but its radiance lingers in golden aspen in the East Meadow.

A springer spaniel is well named. Sadie springs lightly over tall grasses in pursuit of imaginary game. Not imaginary, perhaps, but long gone from this spot. We do see recent deer hoof prints in soft mud that rain has left. Sadie fans back and forth across the trail in true retriever style. She carries a short stick in her mouth which she has insisted on bringing along. Occasionally she drops it at my feet, asking me to throw it for her to retrieve. All this must be genetic; no one has shown her what hunting is all about.

She leads me beyond the pines and into scrub oak (young black oaks.) The smallest trees are still deep red or orange, enhanced by clinging rain drops. Sumac, so brilliant a week ago, has faded into withered strips of soft scarlet. Even twenty-four hours makes a difference in what we see. Yesterday the first frost intensified all colors and etched the still shapely leaf edges in white. Today the colors are subdued and restful.

I wax poetic and decide our walk is like a symphony concert. Reds of sumac and woodbine are violins; dark pines and cedars are basses and bassoons; rust, ochre, and dull orange oaks are cellos; and chartreuse, gold, and coral cherries and maples become flutes.

As we walk back along the river toward the house, the sun is again shining through clouds, lighting up maples and even dull oaks across the river. Lavender, gray, purple, and white clouds are reflected in the early morning calm of the river.

A flock of geese honk their way southward, reminding us winter is not far off. A bluebird sings softly in a nearby oak, bringing thoughts back to summer. If I had been in the house washing dishes with the radio on I wouldn't have known they were there.

❧❧❧

126 Clausen

In 1979, Indian summer came in the middle of November. We went outside in the morning and it seemed like spring. Even the chill of evening couldn't disenchant us as we looked up at a million stars shining in the soft blackness of sky.

"Let's go to Baxter's Hollow! It's too nice a day to waste inside." This very logical invitation from Connie Peckham the next morning was hard to resist, though I had planned to spend the morning at the typewriter.

Baxter's Hollow is nestled into the Baraboo Hills at the end of a long bumpy road. A cheerful little stream dances its way through a valley which is sometimes wide, sometimes narrow, with wooded hills on either side. Occasionally the slope is precipitous and rocky.

"A north slope — what a perfect place for the spring ephemerals!" I remarked.

"Oh, yes," Connie replied, "Right here it's covered with Dutchman's-breeches. And, over there, it's full of hepatica. Look, you can see their liver-shaped leaves all through here. They start to grow late in summer, to get a head start for next year."

Later she showed me where the skunk cabbage grew, and a sunnier corner of the stream that she said would be yellow with marsh marigolds.

"This would be great dragon habitat," I suggested. "Remember the children's story book *My Father's Dragon?* It says dragons love skunk cabbage and marsh marigolds."

What could we find in November woods? Colors are much more subtle, of course. But we saw some ferns, still green as they climbed down a rocky wall. Most rocks were covered with intricately patterned lichen in soft shades of green.

Bright green moss often cushioned our path. One kind that we could identify was called hair caps. It looked like a miniature pine forest but was soft to the touch.

Another glimpse of bright green underfoot proved to be the roundish, paired leaves of partridge berry. "There should be some little red berries," said Connie. "Sure enough, here's one." After that, we saw many.

We forded the stream, incurring only one wet foot (mine) and started back toward the car. "I'd love to climb that hill — there's a great view from the top," said Connie.

The hill was rocky and slippery with dry leaves, so we skirted the base instead. Around the bend, she said, "Let's just go up partway; it looks easy."

Of course, eventually we found ourselves at the top. We admired the fallow fields and woods of Sauk County below us, then stretched out in the sunshine and discussed the oak leaves and acorns around us, concluding we were in a grove of white oaks.

We had to admit it was November. The wet foot was getting chilly and shadows were lengthening. Getting down on those slippery leaves was not easy for Connie, who was very pregnant. "What was I thinking of," I said to myself. "What if she slips and falls. How will I ever get help?"

We made it somehow, and the expedition accomplished the purpose of allaying our spring fever. There was a nice side effect two days later when Connie produced a beautiful baby boy, Matt.

❧❧❧

Sauntering alone can be rewarding, even in a light rain. From inside the house one sees only a brown, damp November world. But this kind of day improves with exploration.

Rain enhances the few spots of color. Four distinct shades of green catch my eye as I walk along. The first two hug the ground, one gray-green, the other chartreuse. Both could be either moss or lichens. Their structure is so minute that I would have to bring a sample indoors and examine it through a magnifying glass to identify it; but my botanical skills will have to become more advanced first.

The next two shades of green I see must be mosses. They are much taller — at least a quarter of an inch. (You do have to think small in the moss and lichen world.) One of the mosses has many small reddish hairs with a spore case at the end of each. Tiny drops of moisture looking like amber jewels rest in some of the spore cases. The stems of the other moss are dark red with many lighter green branches, each branch about a centimeter long. The top resembles an infinitesimal pine cone — perhaps another spore case.

I have been told that, unlike ferns and flowering plants, mosses have no way to carry water through their stems. During a dry spell they become brown and look dead, but a good rain brings their jewel-like color back.

Patches of British soldiers march across the sand and line up on an old fallen log. I am familiar with this gray-green lichen, with stems as much as half an inch tall, culminating in a bright orange-red odd-shaped cap.

Someone who has walked in the meadow on a dry day is often amazed to see so much color appear seemingly out of nowhere after a rain. In 1962, a volcano formed a new island off the coast of Iceland, and twenty years later some friends brought back pictures of mosses and lichens that were already growing there. These plants seem to

128 Clausen

thrive on poor conditions; no wonder they like our dry, sandy east meadow.

❊❊❊

It was a perfect March day — warm sun, little wind, just a touch of chill in the air, a calm river. But it was only January — 1980, to be exact. The Benforados had brought some friends with a ten-year-old son named Chris to walk the riverbank with us.

"I want to see an eagle!" Chris announced firmly.

"We know it's not very likely," his mother said apologetically, "but we've never seen one."

"They have been pretty scarce this year, but we'll see what we can do," I replied.

As we started out we checked trees the beavers had been chewing, just above their home in the riverbank. No sign of fresh beaver teeth marks. If we hadn't seen one swimming upstream from here the other day we would have thought they had moved away.

We walked on along the riverbank. As we got into the tangle of prickly ash that prevails in much of the bottomland, we found a log about eight inches across that had been dragged toward the river. It had been chewed part way through into manageable segments about eighteen inches long. These marks and the chips on the ground were still white.

"So this is where they are coming now for their daily bread," I said. "Look how well worn this path to the river is — but it's not man-made, and it leads only as far as those telltale pointed stumps, probably aspen and box elder."

"Looks like father assigned each child a spot — Jim, you chew here, Susie, a little farther down!" Sally Benforado remarked.

As we made our way with some difficulty through a tangle of trees along the riverbank, Chris spied a big bird soaring over the trees across the river.

"That's a big bird — it must be an eagle!" he shouted.

"Then it must be an immature — its head and tail are dark," I replied.

"Maybe it's a hawk. The head and underparts are light when it turns in the sun," said Joe Benforado.

"That looks too big for a hawk," Sally said.

Norm chimed in: "But I don't think that really flies like an eagle. He does have his wings out perfectly straight when he soars, though."

"He's coming this way, but he's soaring higher and higher," said Chris hopefully.

"Rusty underparts, especially the tail. He must be a red-tail, but he's a big one," Norm said.

We went on, admiring the diaphanous tawny pink skin flaking off a river birch. Later we tried to decide whether a certain small tree with slender yellow buds was a butternut hickory or not.

Suddenly Chris spotted another large bird. Again the adults took turns with their comments.

"It's the same hawk. He came back," suggested Chris' mother.

"No, this is an eagle, I can see the white head!" This time Chris was really excited.

"It is — it really is!" we chorused.

"Yes, that's an eagle. He flies differently — more slowly and majestically," Norm said.

"And see those wings as he soars — absolutely straight. Only the tips turn down a little," added Joe.

Sauntering with a purpose, aimless sauntering; sauntering alone or with friends. We've done them all. I think Thoreau would be pleased.

XV.
Being

Best of all, on the riverbank there's time for just *being*. In December of 1976, our first year of retirement, we arrived home from a ten-week trip to what the weather announcer kept referring to as "bitter cold." We awoke next morning to three or four inches of snow covering the ground and intensifying the tawny colors of grasses and lingering oak leaves.

From the breakfast table we watched two eagles soaring and circling. Their white tails gleamed in the early morning light as they tilted and turned above the open water of the river. Sometimes one would hover purposefully for a moment fifty feet or so above the river, then drop lightly to the surface to catch a small fish in his talons. If successful, he would fly in a big arc to a tall tree nearby to enjoy breakfast. We could scarcely eat ours for the fascination of watching.

Other old friends were at the feeder to greet us. Most numerous were juncos and chickadees. At least one of each species of woodpeckers showed up — hairy, downy, red-bellied and redheaded. Sometimes a large flock of sparrows would come in and take over. They are welcome, too, because they scatter lots of seed for birds like juncos and cardinals who prefer to feed on the ground. When five or six bluejays came in, the smaller birds disappeared. But their handsome coats in shades of blues and grays against the white snow were beautiful enough that we forgave them.

Suddenly the wind chill factor, whatever it was, mattered not at all!

❦❦❦

On a late March day the bitter cold has left, but looking out, I see nothing but trees and bushes still clinging to their stoic winter gray. However, I change my mind while sitting for a half hour in convincingly warm sunshine on the steps overlooking the river. Right under my nose, black raspberry bushes sprawl over the bank with perfect miniature leaves climbing up their stems. Close inspection reveals tiny buds at the tips of cherry, ash, and gray dogwood branches.

A short walk across the meadow to my barometer of spring, and I'm sure: the silver maple is in flower. Now this is not a showy flower at all; from the ground the tips of branches seem to be covered with something fuzzy and red. Like many of nature's miniatures however, each fuzzy red flower is beautiful on close inspection through binoculars.

Sounds of spring are all around me. I hear the self-confident notes of a robin; the reassuring, melodious soft warbling of a bluebird; the almost constant sweet, high-pitched song of goldfinches, punctuated often by a rising inflection that sounds like *swe-e-et?*

From far across the meadow I hear the clear ringing *spring is here, is here!* of a meadow lark. From high in a treetop downstream somewhere comes the distinctive call of the song sparrow, which begins and ends with three notes.

Final proof that spring is here comes inside the house. I swat the first fly of the season.

The colors of spring? Chartreuse leaves against a blue sky.

The smell of spring? Sun on the warm earth, and maybe apple blossoms.

The sounds of spring? The rustle of new aspen leaves when a sudden breeze strikes them; the carefully paired notes of a brown thrasher singing song after song to proclaim his territory; and the hum of the first mosquito as we watch the mating dance of the woodcock at dusk.

The taste of spring? Fresh asparagus, and rhubarb pie!

The feel of spring? It feels like lying in a hammock and looking up at those chartreuse leaves and the sky, and feeling too lazy to write a column today.

❦❦❦

Just what is a perfect June day on the riverbank? First there is a fresh fragrance of the air itself as a light breeze stirs boughs in pines

132　　　　　　　　　　　　Clausen

and oaks. A small wren sings self-importantly in the lowest branch of one of the oaks. Not far away is a clump of yellow puccoon — as brassy as the wren's song.

Hoary alyssum, daisy fleabane, and yarrow sprinkle cooling white through the green meadow. Like a *fleur-de-lis* centered with vivid yellow, I catch sight of the deep blue of a single spiderwort flower, while beyond it lies a whole sea of those bright blossoms with the spidery foliage.

A hawk soars against fleecy clouds, making me feel terribly earthbound. River birch branches bow gracefully to the passing breeze.

Young cedars planted twelve years earlier as a windbreak for the driveway now reach for the sky. Some are decked with an abundance of frosty blueberries.

A crested flycatcher calls lazily from a high perch somewhere, while a cricket sings diligently near the basement window.

A female oriole, softly beautiful in pale orange and brown, explores the woodpile. Finding a piece of string, she tugs until it is free, then flies off to the other side of the house. I cut more string loose, hoping she will return. It seems late for her to be building a nest. Perhaps she is just redecorating.

A song sparrow sings from a treetop on the riverbank. A yellowthroat can be heard down there somewhere in the prickly ash. Loud humming alerts me to a ruby-throated hummingbird at the feeder just outside the porch.

Birds, flowers and trees of the riverbank are all celebrating a perfect June day with us.

❦❦❦

Now that the grass has suddenly decided to grow about half an inch a night, our lawn mower has refused to start and is in for repairs. I find the lawn much more interesting now. Each individual blade of grass has its own stance; the longer ones wave gently in the breeze.

Spiders were busy one night and left a patch of gossamer where I could admire it out the window. Some of the longer grass held it up like the several poles in a circus tent. Suspended an inch or so above this dew-covered creation was an even more filmy-looking piece of spider artistry, fastened by taut "guy wires" to longer blades of grass beyond.

Being human and curious, I had to find some reason for this new structure on my lawn. I concluded it must be one of two things: (1) The fairies put up an extensive circus tent during the night. Or: (2) A fairy bride dropped her veil and train after the wedding.

The reason I couldn't tell which it really was is because I'm not

To Thank a River

sure how big fairies are. This gossamer thing is about eight inches by four inches. But I don't think fairies know about inches.

❦❦❦

Woods across the river look clear and green — a photo image. The river reflects the blue of the sky, and seems to be as deep as the sky is high. The woods reflected in water are a French impressionist painting. It is early morning and the water is quiet, current flowing invisibly.

A crow calls in the distance, a cardinal sings a brief absent-minded song, accompanied by mixed chorus of cicadas and crickets. Otherwise we are alone with our river.

By noon, wind has fractured the surface of the river into small waves, and it no longer looks deep and mysterious. Canoes glide by in twos and threes. Canoers with overnight gear paddle purposefully. Those who carry cases of beer and boom boxes float by, oblivious to the beauty around them.

By the time the sun sets, wind and canoes are gone; the river is ours again. As darkness comes, the afterglow grows more intense. Our river is a deep tangerine well, seen through the lacy black of leaves and tree branches.

A poet would have expressed these thoughts with greater economy of words:

> *The river is a blue mirror*
> *Deep as the sky is high.*
> *The river is a green mirror*
> *Deep as the forest is deep.*
> *In early morning it is ours alone.*
> *Later we must share it*
> *With wind and canoes.*
> *After sunset it is ours again,*
> *A deep tangerine well*
> *Seen through black*
> *Silhouettes of trees.*

❦❦❦

The river on a summer weekend is a noisy, companionable, friendly place. Wooden paddles in the hands of beginners clank against aluminum canoes. Laughter spills out from pink bodies turning redder in July sun. Shouts of private jokes pass from canoe to canoe.

From far upstream I hear the sound of a boom box. After what seems a long time it appears, ensconced in one of five canoes floating abreast. One pink body is being towed in an inner tube.

The flotilla finally disappears downstream. It is again possible to hear crickets chirping in the noonday sun, and the rattle of a kingfisher as he dives from an overhanging tree.

As I watch and listen my imagination wanders to the same scene in midwinter.

Summer river, noisy, friendly
Wooden paddles bang canoes.
Laughter floats across the water
Bodies redden in midday sun.
Winter river, silent, majestic
Icy edges, snowy banks
Water mirrors somber trees
Bluejay calling shatters silence.

❊❊❊

At a Thanksgiving Eve church service in Sauk Prairie, Pastor Larry Collins listed some of the things we would be grateful for as we sat down to dinner next day, such as looking out the window at the beautiful November landscape. He said "We all enjoy October when fall colors are at their peak, but I also like November when the dull colors are at their peak."

I sometimes get over-stimulated by the splendor of October, and actually feel a sense of relief when it's over. After that I almost become frustrated trying to describe the great variety of subdued color we have before everything gets etched in dramatic black and white.

Oak leaves are not dull brown. They are tawny to copper to chestnut colors. Red cedar turns to its winter purplish color. White pine trees all have neat little rugs of fallen orange pine needles under them. Clumps of little bluestem are wispy pink. Cudweed (sweet everlasting) is frosty white.

Dainty seedheads and thin curling leaves of switch grass are pale gold. Robust seed heads of bush clover are chocolate brown. Stray milkweed pods are textured gray. Weathered wood is silver to charcoal gray. The East Meadow's anonymous grasses are bleached to a pale gold, accented by coffee-brown sprays of artemisia. Tall tobacco-brown stalks of mullein shiver in the wind.

Scraggly gray bases of river birch trunks grow gracefully upward to become a tawny color that produces pink ruffles. The aspen copse is a uniformly pale ghostly gray.

The river and the sky are seven shades of gray for which I shall not attempt to find names.

To Thank a River

***

The sky is soft, round, pearl-gray clouds and looks like the inside of a clam shell. But in the west a strip of crimson-orange sunset hovers over dark woods on the riverbank. Hot pink in the sky is cooled down to a silky delicate pink reflected in the wintry river.

Chicken soup simmering on the stove delights my senses while I sip tea in a rocker at the window. Sounds of a football game on television indicate that Norm is contented in the next room.

An imperious *chip ... chip ... chip* turns my attention to the bird feeder. A crimson cardinal has come in for a bedtime snack. His grayer mate waits in the background for his departure before she comes in for a few morsels under the feeder.

As I turn my eyes again to the west, colors are fading. A band of clear yellow-green sky has produced a row of pink and lavender bubble-shaped clouds. A phosphorescent blue yard light over someone else's riverbank home appears among the trees. Gray-blue bluffs in the distance contrast with dark woods near the river's edge.

Soon the sky is drained of color; the river is luminescent. The blue light now has a long brilliant trail in the river, taking on more importance as darkness comes. Home always takes on importance as darkness comes.

When darkness is complete, all we'll be able to see in the west is that phosphorescent blue yard light and its long reflection.

***

People often write poems or eloquent prose about the sounds of spring, but few sing of the sounds of autumn. Perhaps that is because there aren't any.

On a perfect Indian summer day, I sit down near the river to look and listen a while. The deep blue sky is mirrored in placid water. We've had strong winds for a couple of days and most of the trees are bare. Across the river only an occasional dull gold birch gleams through dusky outlines of leafless ash and elm trees.

Now and then a bright yellow cherry leaf floats noiselessly down to still-green grass beside me. A junco flies swiftly by with another in close pursuit. Did the mild weather fool them into thinking it was spring? I don't think so. Spring brings an abundance of bird song, but in autumn birds go silently about the business of finding food and shelter and enjoying the sunshine.

The nasal *yank yank* of a nuthatch, who hangs upside down on the suet feeder, punctuates the silence. The soft *chip* of a cardinal as

136   *Clausen*

he comes in to feed is the only other bird song we usually hear these days. It will be several months before the clear melodious whistle of his early spring territorial call is heard. Jays and crows, however, are functioning as usual — the early warning system of the woods.

Far down across the river I hear a dog barking. He sounds forlorn. Did a hunter leave him stranded there? The hum of a car on the road a couple of hundred yards away comes down to the riverbank where I sit. A gun fires somewhere far away, then another.

These are the sounds of autumn. Jays and crows, dogs barking and distant gun shots. I don't hear the honking of Canada geese today; but I see white gulls wheeling without sound against blue sky. The setting sun rests now on mahogany colored oak trees that refuse to give up their leaves yet.

The silence is golden.

❧❧❧

Sometime in November the bland weather of fall comes to a halt. There have been days of quiet grayness and fog, punctuated occasionally by golden Indian summer sunshine. Sometimes during the gray periods the biggest excitement of the day is watching trees across the river slowly and mysteriously emerge from morning fog.

Eventually on a dark evening we hear the welcome sound of wind rising in trees around the house. This means a change is coming, quickening the blood and the spirits. The next day there is no morning fog. Trees on Blackhawk Ridge stand out in fine detail against the morning. The sky, no dull gray bowl today, is boiling with round ominous-looking clouds which have ragged, dark gray edges. The thermometer registers 30 degrees colder than yesterday morning.

On the river a strong wind out of the west sends whitecaps to do battle with the current, which is determined to go the other way. The sky begins to spit snow, and a trace of white accumulates on the feeding table and the fallen tree where birds like to perch.

High in the sky a score of Canada geese gather themselves into a "V" and head south. A flock of ducks come through. They seem confused about which way to go, but finally gather themselves into some order and veer off to the south.

There is a certain urgency about the feeding of many small birds on and beneath our feeders. Chickadees and nuthatches dart in for a snack and quickly disappear. Bluejays and sparrows are more deliberate and more numerous. Juncos and goldfinches prefer to concentrate their activities at the feeding table. A tufted titmouse puts in an appearance. Even a tardy bluebird has a few seeds before departing for a little warmer climate.

When the large gray squirrel ambles in, birds scatter. Our ground squirrel is nowhere to be seen, doubtless snug in his burrow for the winter.

The next day the sun shines; the north wind is cold but doesn't fight with the current — only urges the river faster downstream. Suddenly my eye catches a flash of red on the water upstream. Two red kayaks appear, drifting with the wind and current. They stay close together like a catamaran. The two passengers are so well wrapped in down jackets and hoods that any identification is impossible. Against the icy blue water they make a beautiful if incongruous picture. Evidently some humans too are stirred into action by this preview of winter.

❧❧❧

This is our coldest morning to date. Mist rises off the river in great white clouds, revealing that thick white hoarfrost has decked trees across the river in bridal finery.

A few gulls fly joyously in spite of the cold. Eventually a large flock — there must be a hundred — circles over the river in front of us. As they fly higher, their white wings gleam in the light of the sun just rising over Blackhawk Ridge behind us.

As the sun climbs, light creeps lower on the scene before us. First, sunlight reaches treetops, then whole trees, snow-covered banks, and finally the river itself. About this time an eagle flaps its majestic way downstream. Its great size and dark wings contrast with the slender black-tipped, white-winged gulls in their graceful flight. Next a huge dark immature eagle makes its way into our view, circles once, and swoops down for a fish.

Watching morning unfold on the riverbank is a great antidote for the news we have heard earlier on the radio, most of which was depressing. The world of people contains much uncertainty and misery. In contrast, the world of nature seems dependable and well organized. We can count on the river to continue flowing by, at least one pair of cardinals to fly in for breakfast, bluebirds and barn swallows to return in spring. Just watching the miracle of flight in such contrasting creatures as a chickadee and a bald eagle is reassuring.

❧❧❧

People who live on rivers become philosophical. They tend to sit and stare at the water flowing endlessly by and one of two things happens: either they begin to think profound thoughts, or else become mesmerized and stop thinking at all.

A writer named Tim Palmer put it this way: "There is a kind of magnetism that rivers exert over people: we love water, especially when it is animated. The stream churns, riffles, hisses onto a sandy beach... or it can run silently and peacefully, soothing us with its serenity. Yet

138 Clausen

in a river's grasp is the ability to sculpt and shape continents and house entire ecosystems."

Professor Emeritus Robert Najem of the University of Wisconsin-Madison describes the Oriental attitude toward water this way: "It serves to distract the individual from worldly cares. The rhythmic flow of water helps him to detach himself from the physical world and lose himself in a spiritual one."

Our river does all of these things for us. Stan Nichols, a Madison naturalist, compares the Wisconsin River to a person's lifetime. "It starts life in the North Woods, running wild and free, as a spirited youth. During middle age it works hard, providing energy and resources to people and industry." (There are twenty-six dams.) "Toward the end of its journey, responsibility is shed; it travels with the relaxed freedom of respected maturity, contemplating its wild environment with serenity."

So we chose to live on the relaxed segment, contemplating its wild environment with at least a semblance of serenity. Norm was more relaxed than I, looking forward with interest and enthusiasm to whatever each day might bring. Hopefully it would be a good game of golf, or an invigorating session with the chain saw making fuel for our faithful wood stove, or a quick game of horseshoes with Richard. He often remarked, "I've had my three score years and ten; I figure every day from now on is a bonus day."

I on the other hand became more involved in the community. I was also more determined and diligent in my pursuit of the secrets of nature with which our twenty-five acres was so generously supplied.

❊❊❊

We named our home *Endlichheim*. Loosely translated from the German this means final home. For one of us, at least, it was. This book is based on columns I wrote for the *Sauk Prairie Star* between July 1975 and June 1993. The following column appeared about six weeks later:

The day my last column appeared, June 17, was the day in which one split second changed my life forever. After a three-day vigil in the hospital, I came home to a house which was strangely empty, although it was filled with children and grandchildren.

Those three long days had been cloudy and rainy, but the next morning dawned bright and clear. Curt raised the flag to half-mast, where it remained for one week. We found that the river had been weeping with us; it was full to the banks and running over. Grandchildren went swimming at the bottom of the steps, over land that was normally a grassy playground.

Cardinals, brown thrashers, catbirds and rose-breasted grosbeaks found time to cheer us with their songs, even though they were busy raising young. Soon the mulberry tree was alive with adult birds, carrying home berries to feed their fledglings.

The restoring prairie began to blossom with brown-eyed Susans in new places; the purple prairie clover that appeared only two years ago had many blossoms. Purple spears of leadplant on one side of the upper river path, and spiky white Culver's root on the other, were more spectacular than ever.

As the river slowly went down to a normal summer level, we found ourselves as slowly healing from the loss of a husband, father, and grandfather. Our home on the riverbank will never be the same. But the birds are still singing, the prairie is still blooming, trees are providing benevolent shade, and watching the river flow by brings solace.

Epilogue

The river frequently brought us gifts. The log that once came to rest in full view of the living room windows immediately became the favorite haunt of as many as twenty turtles. One year, directly in the path of the setting sun, we had a Japanese bridge — a log which formed a perfect span, then disappeared again into the water.

I'm sure the Chinese elm close to the shore is a gift from the river, the seed of a tree from someone's upstream yard. Occasionally in the fall we are treated to a few breathtakingly beautiful cardinal flowers, also close to the water. They must be washed out by the next spring's flooding, however, because they don't appear every year.

One day we had another kind of gift — a "recyclable, reusable, hot or cold" plastic mug from McDonald's! Sun and sand had washed it pretty well, so a little more soap and hot water judiciously applied made it indeed useful. Of course we also get unwanted gifts, like empty soda cans, plastic cups, and so on. We faithfully gather these and recycle what we can.

To be sure, the most valuable gift of the river is just the privilege of living beside it daily. Trees on the opposite shore slowly emerging from morning fog. The moon setting over the river on an early winter morning. White gulls performing a ballet against a cloudless sky. An October blue sky reflected in perfectly still water. The excitement of a west wind from Ferry Bluff whipping up whitecaps. And the sunsets! Norm's favorite view was a sunset reflected in the river and viewed through leafless trees.

How does one say thank you to a river?

Bibliography

Following is a list of the sources I frequently use when I write my columns. Many of them are quoted in this book:

Courtenay, Booth and Zimmerman, James Hall, *Wildflowers and Weeds,* Von Nostrand Reinhold Company, New York:1972.

Ehrlich, Paul R., et. al., *The Birder's Handbook,* Simon & Schuster, New York:1988.

Gibbons, Euell, *Stalking the Wild Asparagus,* Davie McKay Company, New York:1962.

Harrison, Hal H., *A Field Guide to Birds' Nests,* Houghton Mifflin Company, Boston:1975.

Jackson, H.T., *Mammals of Wisconsin,* University of Wisconsin Press, Madison, Wis.:1961.

Kirt, Russell R., *Prairie Plants of Northern Illinois,* Stipes Publishing Company, Champaign, Ill.:1989.

Mossman, Michael J. and Lange, Kenneth I., *Breeding Birds of the Baraboo Hills, Wisconsin,* Wisconsin Department of Natural Resources and Wisconsin Society of Ornithology, Madison, Wis.:1982.

Murie, Olaus J., *A Field Guide to Animal Tracks,* Houghton Mifflin Company, Boston:1954.

Nuzzo, Victoria, *Our Native Plants,* The Capital Times, Madison, Wis.:1977.

Peterson Roger Tory and McKenny, Margaret, *A Field Guide to Wildflowers of Northeastern and Northcentral North America,* Houghton Mifflin Company, Boston:1968.

Peterson, Roger Tory, *Field Guide to the Birds East of the Rockies,* Houghton Mifflin Company, Boston:1980.

Petrides, George A., *A Field Guide to Trees and Shrubs,* Houghton Mifflin Company, Boston:1972.

Pough, Richard H., *Audubon Land Bird Guide,* Doubleday, Garden City, N.Y.:1946.

Pough, Richard H., *Audubon Water Bird Guide,* Doubelday, Garden City, N.Y.:1951.

Robbins, Chandler S., et. al., *Golden Guide to Birds of North America,* Western Publishing Company, Racine, Wis.:1983.

Robbins, Samuel J., Jr., *Wisconsin Birdlife,* University of Wisconsin Press, Madison, Wis.:1991.

Runkel, Sy and Roosa, Dean, *Wildflowers of the Tallgrass Prairie,*

Iowa State University Press, Ames, Iowa:1989.

Smith, J. Robert and Smith, Beatrice, *The Prairie Garden,* University of Wisconsin Press, Madison, Wis.:1980.

Stahlmaster, Mark, *The Bald Eagle,* Universe Books, New York:1987.

Temple, Stanley A. and Cary, John R., *Wisconsin Birds: A Seasonal and Geographical Guide,* University of Wisconsin Press, Madison, Wis.:1987.